Elementary
Vocabulary

B J Thomas

Nelson

Thomas Nelson and Sons Ltd
Nelson House Mayfield Road
Walton-on-Thames Surrey KT12 5PL UK

51 York Place
Edinburgh EH1 3JD UK

Thomas Nelson (Hong Kong) Ltd
Toppan Building 10/F
22A Westlands Road
Quarry Bay Hong Kong

© BJ Thomas 1990

First published by Edward Arnold,
a division of Hodder and Stoughton Ltd

ISBN 0-340-52952-0

This edition first published by
Thomas Nelson and Sons Ltd 1990

ISBN 0-17-556082-X
NPN 9 8 7 6 5 4 3

Printed in Great Britain
by Bell and Bain Ltd, Glasgow

Contents

Introduction

Topics

How To Do Things

Related Word Groups

Word Building

Idioms

Miscellaneous

Key....62

INTRODUCTION

Elementary Vocabulary is for students who are doing a beginner's course in English and wish to check and expand their basic vocabulary. Students at intermediate level will also find it useful for checking and testing themselves. The book presents essential words from a variety of common, everyday topic areas, vocabulary which all learners will need to know at an early stage of their studies. The varied and enjoyable exercises include gap-filling, matching and word-building.

To the student

If you are studying without a teacher, do not simply go through the book 'filling in the blanks'. When you learn new words, practise them and note the spelling before you do other exercises. It is not enough simply to *understand* new words: if you want the words to become part of your active vocabulary, you must *use* them in conversation, composition or letters.

To the teacher

Elementary Vocabulary is divided into six sections, each presenting words on a different basis of selection and in a variety of exercises in which words are contextualized. The first two sections, *Topics* and *How to Do Things*, contain words and phrases in basic topic areas such as *shopping* and *using a cassette player*, and include items useful for students writing about or discussing a particular topic. The third section, *Related Word Groups*, contains sets of essential adjectives, verbs and nouns which students should know before proceeding to the intermediate level. The fourth section, *Word Building*, encourages students to be aware of how words are formed and should help them to deduce the meanings of unknown words by recognizing common patterns in word formation. The fifth section, *Idioms*, is an introduction to the everyday idiomatic usage of common vocabulary. The sixth section, *Miscellaneous*, is a reference section giving invaluable, practical information on the most common abbreviations and rules of spelling.

Elementary Vocabulary can be used in a variety of ways. Exercises will probably be most effective if students do them only after the subject matter has been introduced and explained. The book should not be used to give students a series of mechanical tests. Exercises can be done as pair or group activities in class, followed by discussion or other creative tasks in which the students are required to use the words they have learnt. Simpler exercises can be done as homework, after suitable class preparation or with the aid of the key or a dictionary.

Note: a companion volume, *Intermediate Vocabulary*, also contains a number of exercises suitable for elementary learners and these exercises will supplement the material in this book.

TOPICS

The Weather

1 Match each of the following words with the correct picture.

cloud	fog	mist	sun	snow	wind	rain	forecast
g	b	c	h	e	f	d	a

2 Put each of the following adjectives in the correct space in the passage below.

wet	hot	freezing	cold	clear
dry	mild	changeable	warm	cloudy

I always watch the weather <u>forecast</u> on television to see what tomorrow's weather will be like. In England the weather changes very often. It's very (a) changeable Sometimes it rains for a day or two, but after the (b) wet weather, often with noisy <u>thunderstorms</u>, it is sometimes (c) dry for a long time, with no rain at all. On some days the sun shines and the sky is (d) clear , but on other days it is so (e) cloudy you can't see the sun. English summers aren't usually very (f) hot but the <u>temperature</u> usually <u>reaches</u> 25°, so it's quite (g) warm . In winter it is sometimes quite (h) mild and pleasant but sometimes it's very (i) cold or even (j) freezing. The English climate isn't very good for holidays but it makes the countryside green.

3 Finish each sentence on the left below with the correct verb on the right.

(a) We get wet when it   (1) shines.
(b) When it's very cold, everything   (2) rains.
(c) Children enjoy playing games when it (3) blows.
(d) It's cold in England when a north wind (4) freezes.
(e) It's warm and pleasant when the sun (5) pours.
(f) When it rains very heavily, it   (6) snows.

4 What's the weather like in your country?

✓ Going Shopping

1 Match each of the following words with the correct item in the picture.

shelves   **customers**   **check-out**   **cashier**   **trolley**
queue   **assistant**   **till**   **manager**   **basket**

2 Put each of the following words or phrases in the correct space in the passage below.

pay   **push**   **find**   **spend**   **take**
buy   **sell**   **need**   **complain**   **look for**

I love shopping. I love looking round the shops and seeing all the things
and all the people. My friends say I like to (a) _spend_ money. It's
probably true. There's a very good supermarket near me. They have
everything you (b) _need_ for your house. If you want a tin of sardines,
a tube of toothpaste, a box of chocolates, a carton of milk, a packet of
biscuits, a bottle of beer or a jar of jam, you can (c) _buy_ it at the
supermarket. They (d) _____ everything. If you want a lot of things,
you can use a trolley and (e) _push_ it in front of you. If you don't want
much, you can use a small basket. Then (f) _____ the things you want.
If you can't (g) _find_ them on the shelves, ask an assistant for help.
When you see what you want, you just (h) _____ it from the shelves
and put it in the trolley. When you have everything, you must stand in
the queue at the check-out to (i) _pay_. Give your money to the
cashier. He or she will put it in the till and give you your change. If
there is anything wrong, if the service isn't good, customers can (j)
_____ to the manager. Our supermarket is super.

3 Put the correct word or phrase from the following list in each space below.

from   round   in front of   for   on   at   in   to

(a) Before I buy, I look _____ the shop.
(b) I must buy some things _____ my house.
(c) You can buy almost everything _____ the supermarket.
(d) I pushed the trolley _____ me.
(e) There's some nice fruit _____ that shelf.
(f) I asked an assistant _____ some help.
(g) I took some biscuits _____ the shelf.
(h) I put the bottles _____ my trolley.
(i) I had to wait _____ a queue.
(j) I gave the correct money _____ the cashier.

4 Match each of the following words with the correct picture.

jar   carton   tin   bottle   tube   box   packet

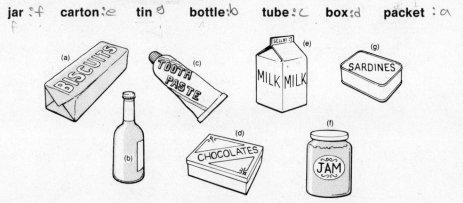

In which of the above containers do we usually buy the following things? Sometimes more than one answer is possible.

E.g. soup: tin or packet

(h) wine	(k) fruit juice	(n) fruit salad	(q) cigarettes
(i) matches	(l) face cream	(o) honey	(r) paint
(j) glue	(m) marmalade	(p) sugar	(s) rice

5 On the left below are phrases we often use in shops. Match each one to the correct assistant's reply on the right.

(a) Can I try this jacket on?

(b) Does this jacket suit me?

(c) Does this jacket fit me?

(d) Can I pay by cheque?

(e) I'm afraid I only have a £10 note.

(f) Can I exchange this?

(g) Can I have my money back?

(1) Of course, if you have some kind of bank card.

(2) I'm afraid we don't give refunds.

(3) Certainly. There's a changing room over there.

(4) It's a little too long. Try a smaller size.

(5) If you have a receipt.

(6) That's alright. I can change it.

(7) Yes, it's just the right colour and style for you.

Work

1 Match each word or phrase on the left below with the correct phrase on the right.

(a) wages   (1) certificates and exams passed
(b) skills   (2) a talk with a company about a possible job
(c) experience   (3) the times when you work
(d) qualifications   (4) points in your character (politeness, honesty etc.)
(e) interview   (5) abilities, things you can do (type, drive etc.)
(f) hours   (6) work of the same type you have done before
(g) personal qualities   (7) money you get, usually hourly or weekly ('salary' is usually monthly or annually)

2 Put each of the words on the left in Exercise 1 above, in the correct space in the following conversation.

Valerie: Hello, I'm Valerie Woods. I've come for an (a) _____ for a job as a secretary.

Mr Watts: Oh yes, Miss Woods. Please take a seat. Well, have you done office work before? Have you any (b) _____ ?

Valerie: Well, I'm afraid I haven't. I've just left college. But I have some (c) _____. Here are my typing and shorthand certificates.

Mr Watts: Good. Have you any other (d) _____ ? Can you use a computer?

Valerie: No, but I speak French and Spanish.

Mr Watts: Good. Your teachers tell us you're very careful and you get on well with other people, so there's no problem about your (e) _____. In fact you seem very suitable.

Valerie: Thank you. Can I just make sure of one or two points? I believe the (f) _____ are £150 a week. Is that right?

Mr Watts: Yes, that's right. And the (g) _____ are nine to five, Monday to Friday. Well, we'd like to have you, Miss Woods.

Valerie: Thank you very much. I think the job will suit me very well.

3 Finish each sentence on the left with the correct phrase on the right.

(a) He found   (1) in his work.
(b) He was   (2) an advertisement.
(c) He applied   (3) his work very interesting.
(d) He answered   (4) at science and mathematics.
(e) He had   (5) honest and hard-working.
(f) He was interested   (6) to the company for a job.
(g) He was very good   (7) a lot of experience.

4 Match each job in the following list with the correct picture.

scientist   waiter   porter   businessman   journalist
librarian   priest   lawyer   carpenter   labourer
secretary   farmer   actress   mechanic   footballer

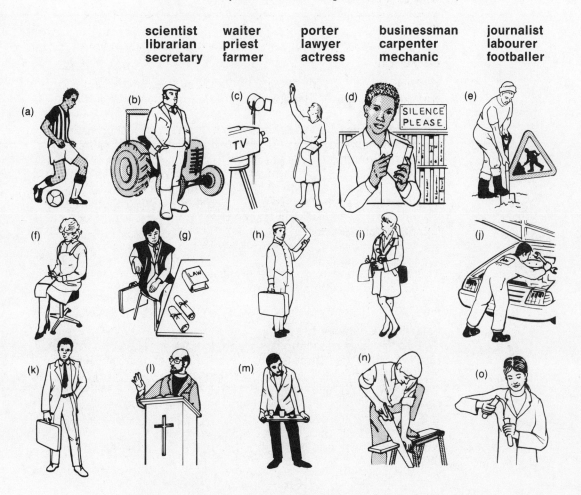

5 We often use the following adjectives to describe different kinds of jobs. Using a dictionary to find the meanings if necessary, give one or two examples of jobs from Exercise 4 for each adjective.

E.g. badly-paid (with low wages or salary): labourer, porter

(a) interesting   (c) mentally hard   (e) exciting
(b) boring   (d) physically hard   (f) well-paid

6 Describe

(a) a job that you have had
(b) the job you have now
(c) the job that you would like to have in the future

Education

1 Put each of the following words in the correct space in the passage below.

staff	primary school	pupils
learn	play-school	terms
start	compulsory	mixed

Bobby's parents decided to send him to a (a) _____ when he was three. They wanted him to (b) _____ to play with other children. In Britain children must, by law, (c) _____ school at the age of five. Education is (d) _____ from then. Bobby's first real school was the (e) _____. There are three (f) _____ a year and holidays at Christmas, Easter and in summer. The (g) _____ are boys and girls together, so it's a (h) _____ school. The teachers on the (i) _____ are young and friendly. Bobby likes the school.

2 Instructions as above.

take	specialize	state school
pass	marks	private school
fail	subjects	secondary school

Sally has just started her new school at the age of 11. There are different kinds of school from this age, but the general word for them is (a) _____. Sally's school is a government school, usually called a (b) _____. Some parents pay to send their children to a (c) _____. At first Sally will take a lot of different (d) _____ (history, English, chemistry etc.) but, after a few years, she'll begin to (e) _____ in things she is good at and interested in. Then she'll (f) _____ some exams. If she can (g) _____ a number of exams with good (h) _____ (A,B,C), it will help her to get a good job. Of course she hopes she doesn't (i) _____.

3 Instructions as above.

courses	last	degree
studies	graduate	grant
student	keen	fees

Harry is 21. He passed his school exams with good marks and left school at 19. Now he's at university. He's a (a) _____ and he receives a (b) _____ from the state to help him pay the university (c) _____ and his personal expenses. He is very (d) _____ on his subject, mathematics, and it will be useful to him in the future. He works hard and enjoys his (e) _____ . University (f) _____ in Britain usually (g) _____ for three years. After this, Harry hopes to (h) _____ . A good (i) _____ will get him a good job.

4 Instructions as above.

mark   **strict**   **graduate**
prepare   **classes**   **teacher training college**
behave   **lessons**   **homework**

Betty is 35 and she's a teacher of English in a state secondary school. She's a (a) _____ of Sussex University and has a degree in English Literature. When she graduated, she first worked in an office but she was very bad at typing and soon got bored with the job. She decided she wanted to teach, so she went to a (b) _____ . She teaches six different (c) _____ of children between the ages of 12 and 18. The pupils enjoy her (d) _____ , but she finds it hard work. She gives the children a lot of (e) _____ to do, and every evening she has to (f) _____ it and to (g) _____ for the next day. One problem is that the children in Betty's school don't (h) _____ very well. They're often impolite. Betty and the other teachers have to be very (i) _____ with them.

5 Put the correct word from the following list in each space below.

from   in   with   between   of   at   to   on

(a) Bobby started school _____ the age of five.
(b) They have a holiday _____ Christmas.
(c) There's a holiday _____ the summer, too.
(d) The teachers _____ the staff are very young.
(e) Sally goes _____ a secondary school.
(f) She'll probably pass _____ good marks.
(g) Harry's _____ university.
(h) He gets a grant _____ the state.
(i) Mathematics will be very useful _____ him _____ the future.
(j) Betty's a teacher _____ English.
(k) She's a graduate _____ Sussex University.
(l) She has a degree _____ English Literature.
(m) Her pupils are _____ 12 and 18.
(n) She's very strict _____ them.

6 Use complete sentences to say what school subjects you are, or were

(a) good at.   (c) interested in.   (e) keen on.
(b) bad at.   (d) bored with.

You can choose from the following list of subjects, using a dictionary if necessary to find the meanings.

biology   **art**   **history**   **literature**
mathematics   **chemistry**   **languages**   **computers**
sport   **physics**   **geography**

7 Use complete sentences to answer the following questions about schools in your country and your own education.

(a) Do children usually go to play-schools? Are they free?
(b) Between what ages is education compulsory?
(c) When do you have holidays?
(d) How long are they?
(e) What different kinds of secondary schools are there?
(f) Are they mixed schools?
(g) Are there many private schools?
(h) Did you specialize in certain subjects at school? Which ones?
(i) Did you take any exams? What were the results?
(j) What did you do, or what would you like to do, at university?
(k) How long do university courses last?
(l) Do students receive grants?
(m) Do you have to be a graduate to teach in a state school?
(n) Did you do, or do you do, a lot of homework at school?
(o) Do pupils behave well at school?

Money

1 Put each of the following verbs in the correct space in the passage below.

pay	spend	save	open	lend
pay back	earn	afford	owe	borrow

Joy: Pam, I'm in trouble. I (a) _____ £200 a week from my job, but I need to (b) _____ about £250 a week just on basic things like food, rent and fares. I can't make ends meet on £200. I've got to (c) _____ some money. Can you help?

Pam: Yes, OK. I'm quite well-off at the moment. I can (d) _____ you £100. Here you are. But why don't you (e) _____ a bank account? It's very simple. Then you can (f) _____ a little bit every week, and you won't be so hard-up.

Joy: Pam, I haven't got enough money to put in a bank account! I can't (g) _____ my gas and electricity bills. I can't (h) _____ to go on holiday. I'm not just a bit hard-up. I've got no money at all. I'm broke! Anyway, thanks for your help. I promise to (i) _____ the £100 next month. I don't like to be in debt. I won't forget. I now (j) _____ you £100.

2 Put each of the following words or phrases in the correct space in the sentences below.

broke	hard-up	in debt	well-off	make ends meet

(a) She earns a lot of money. She's very _____ .
(b) He never has a lot of money. He can't afford luxuries. He's always _____ .
(c) I'll have to get an extra job in the evenings. I can't _____ on my salary.
(d) I'm sorry I can't lend you any money. I haven't got any. I'm absolutely _____ .
(e) He's _____ . He owes money to me and to the bank too.

3 Put the correct word from the following list in each space below.

     in   **from**   **on**

(a) He earns £150 _____ his evening job.
(b) I spend £8 a week _____ fares.
(c) She has to make ends meet _____ £500 a month.
(d) I put some money _____ my bank account.

4 First match each item on the left below with its meaning on the right. Then divide the words into two groups under the headings 'Income' (money you receive) and 'Expenditure' (money you spend).

(a) taxes	(1) cinema, theatre, restaurant meals etc.
(b) pocket-money	(2) money for transport, e.g. bus, train, taxi
(c) salary	(3) part of income paid to government
(d) entertainment	(4) money parents give children every week
(e) rent	(5) money from work, usually hourly or weekly
(f) interest	(6) money for lighting, heating in your house
(g) wages	(7) money from work, usually monthly or annually
(h) pension	(8) e.g. 6% a year from your money in the bank
(i) fares	(9) money for people who stop work at the age of about 60
(j) gas and electricity bills	(10) weekly or monthly payments for your room, flat or house

Can you think of any more items of income or expenditure?

5 Answer the following questions using complete sentences.

(a) What do you spend your money on?
(b) How much does a doctor earn in your country?
(c) Do you save any money? If so, how (bank, cash)?
(d) Is it easy to open a bank account in your country? How much do you need to start?
(e) Do you owe money? Who to? When will you pay back the money?
(f) Is there something you want to do but can't afford to?
(g) Do you often lend money? Who do you lend it to?
(h) Do you often borrow money? Who do you borrow it from?
(i) Are you in debt, broke, hard-up or well-off?
(j) How much do you need to make ends meet?
(k) Do people in your country receive a state pension when they are old? How old are they when they begin to receive it?
(l) What bills do you have to pay?
(m) How much pocket-money did you receive when you were 12 years old?
(n) In your country, what percentage of a person's income is taken in taxes?

A Life

1 Put each of the following verbs in the correct space in the passage below.

bring up	**leave**	**settle down**	**educate**	**move**
was born	**join**	**come from**	**grow up**	**become**

Interviewer: Freddie, you're England's number one footballer. Tell us about your early life. Where were you born?

Freddie Fox: Well, I (a) _____ in the North of England 22 years ago. I (b) _____ a small, quiet village. It was a nice place for a child to (c) _____ and in the future I'd like to (d) _____ my own children in the country.

Interviewer: And where did you go to school?

Freddie Fox: Well, education is sometimes a problem in the country. My parents couldn't (e) _____ me themselves so I had to travel several miles to the nearest school. But then my father had to (f) _____ to London for his work.

Interviewer: And you were invited to (g) _____ Arsenal Football Club.

Freddie Fox: That's right. I was 16 so I was able to (h) _____ school and (i) _____ a professional footballer.

Interviewer: And what about the future?

Freddie Fox: Well, I don't know. I'm still young. I'll get married. I'll play football as long as I can. When I stop, I hope to get a job as a club manager. And finally I'd like to (j) _____ in the North of England again.

2 Put the correct word from the following list in each space below.

as	**in**	**at**	**from**

(a) He's _____ the army.
(b) He was born _____ the South of England.
(c) I come _____ Newcastle.
(d) _____ the future I'd like to be a doctor.
(e) I live _____ the country, not the town.
(f) _____ the moment I'm a secretary.
(g) I'll leave my job _____ a few years.
(h) She wants to get a job _____ a nurse.

3 Finish each sentence on the left with the correct phrase on the right.

(a) To be a soldier	(1) you join the fire-brigade.
(b) To be a sailor	(2) you join the post office.
(c) To be a fireman	(3) you join the Civil Service.
(d) To be a policeman or policewoman	(4) you join the army.
(e) To be a postman	(5) you join the navy.
(f) To be a Civil Servant (in a government office)	(6) you join the police force.

4 Answer the following questions about yourself using complete sentences. You can sometimes use the phrases 'in 1978' or 'when I was 17' etc.

(a) Where do you come from? (village, town, region or country)
(b) Where were you born?
(c) Who were you brought up by?
(d) Where did you grow up?
(e) Did your family move? If so, where to?
(f) Where were you educated?
(g) When did you start school?
(h) When did you leave school? Or when will you leave school?
(i) When did you get married? Or when would you like to get married?
(j) What did you do when you left school? Or what will you do when you leave school?
(k) What would you like to do in the future?
(l) Where would you like to settle down?

5 Using words from the exercises above (with verbs in the past tense) describe the lives of the following people.

(a)

Yoko Tanaka	
1964	Born Tokyo, Japan
1967	Parents died, lived with aunt
1970–82	School
1975	Aunt moved to Kyoto with Yoko
1982–86	Kyoto University
1986–	Civil Servant

(b)

Oscar Gonzalez	
1937	Born Madrid, Spain, lived with parents
1942–53	School
1953–65	Navy
1965–75	Police force (in Madrid)
1975	Married
1975–	Security guard (in Barcelona)

6 Describe your own life.

Sport

1   Match each word on the left below with the correct phrase on the right.

(a) team	(1) someone who plays a sport, e.g. a footballer
(b) player	(2) number of goals or points each player or team has
(c) amateur	(3) group of sportsmen who play together, e.g. eleven footballers
(d) professional	(4) person who controls a game
(e) spectator	(5) someone who plays a sport as a paid job
(f) crowd	(6) game, e.g. of football
(g) referee	(7) someone who plays a sport only for enjoyment, not money
(h) match	(8) group of people who watch a sporting event
(i) score	(9) person who watches a sporting event

2   Put each of the following verbs in the correct space in the passage below.

win   lose   draw   train   beat   play   score

I love football. I don't just like to watch it. I like to (a) _____ , too. I belong to a team. Of course it's not my job. We're just amateurs, not professionals. Not many people come to watch. We just have a small crowd. In fact, there are sometimes more players than spectators! We have a game every Saturday, but we (b) _____ together every Tuesday and Thursday evening to prepare and keep fit. We're quite a good team. We (c) _____ most matches. We only (d) _____ a few, and sometimes we (e) _____ (for example, last Saturday the score was 2:2). Next Saturday our match is against a very good team, but I think we'll (f) _____ them, and if I'm lucky I'll (g) _____ a goal or two. Oh, we have a problem. Do you know much about football? Would you like to run up and down in a black shirt and shorts? Our referee has broken his leg. Would you like a job?

3   In most sports, a score of 0 (zero) is called 'nil', but in tennis and table-tennis it's called 'love'. A score of 1:1, 2:2 etc. (a 'draw') is called 'one all', 'two all' etc. How do we say the following scores?

football
(a) 2:0
(b) 4:4
(c) 0:0

tennis/table-tennis
(d) 30:0
(e) 15:15
(f) 0:15

4   Match each of the following sports with the correct picture opposite.

skiing	cycling	basketball
boxing	horse-riding	volley-ball
badminton	tennis	baseball
hockey	table-tennis	cricket
fishing	golf	skating
motor-racing	running	swimming
rugby	football	shooting

5 Can you find the following sporting items in the pictures below?

(1) **boxing glove**	(11) **cricket bat**	(21) **football**
(2) **running track**	(12) **helmet**	(22) **baseball glove**
(3) **racing car**	(13) **baseball bat**	(23) **net**
(4) **pistol**	(14) **baseball cap**	(24) **swimsuit**
(5) **skis**	(15) **skate**	(25) **badminton racket**
(6) **shuttlecock**	(16) **target**	(26) **golf club**
(7) **basketball**	(17) **goal**	(27) **rugby ball**
(8) **running shoe**	(18) **hockey stick**	(28) **basket**
(9) **horse**	(19) **fishing rod**	(29) **boxing ring**
(10) **goggles**	(20) **tennis racket**	(30) **bicycle**

6 Which sport do you like best, and why?

Free Time and Holidays

In each space (a) in the three passages below put the word from the following group (a) which best suits the person in the picture. Then do the same for (b), (c) etc.

(a) cultural things / parties / the open air
(b) sociable / serious / active
(c) classical music / sport / dancing
(d) meeting people / nature / reading
(e) concerts / clubs / sporting events
(f) libraries / the countryside / discos
(g) go by plane / hitch-hike / take a train
(h) hotel / youth hostels / camp sites
(i) learn about other countries / have a good time / be close to nature
(j) sunbathe / go for walks / visit historical places

1 I love (a) _____ . People say I'm (b) _____ . I like (c) _____ and
(d) _____ so I often go to (e) _____ and (f) _____ . On holiday I
(g) _____ and stay at a nice (h) _____ in Spain. I want to (i) _____ .
Every day I (j) _____ on the beach.

2 I'm keen on (a) _____ . I'm a bit (b) _____ . My hobbies are
(c) _____ and (d) _____ so I spend a lot of time at (e) _____ and
(f) _____ . Holidays? Well, I usually (g) _____ to save money and stay
at (h) _____ abroad because I want to (i) _____ . I (j) _____ there.

3 I'm very fond of (a) _____ . I'm a very (b) _____ person. I enjoy
(c) _____ and (d) _____ so I love all (e) _____ and also (f) _____ .
Every summer my friends and I (g) _____ somewhere and sleep in our
tents at (h) _____ . We prefer to (i) _____ . We (j) _____ .

4 Put the correct word from the following list in each space below.

on	at	to	by	of	about

(a) I often go _____ discos and parties.
(b) We stayed _____ a cheap hotel.
(c) She sunbathes _____ the beach.
(d) I'm very keen _____ music.
(e) I spend a lot of time _____ concerts.
(f) I often go _____ concerts.
(g) He stays _____ youth hostels.
(h) He wants to learn _____ other countries.
(i) I'm very fond _____ the open air.
(j) We stayed _____ a camp-site.
(k) They prefer to live close _____ nature.
(l) I'm going there _____ plane.

5 Fill in the table to show the advantages of different types of transport and accommodation. The first one is done for you as an example. (Note: you can use one tick or two.)

	transport					accommodation				
	hitch-hiking	going by car	going by coach	going by train	going by plane	luxury hotel	cheap hotel	youth hostel	camp-site	staying with friends
It's cheap	✓✓									
It's comfortable										
You feel free to do as you like	✓									
It's interesting	✓									
No need to plan or book	✓✓									
No language problems abroad										
It's quick										
It's safe, not dangerous										

6 Say what you think of the free-time activities on the right below, using the phrases on the left.

I love
I'm (not) interested in
I (don't) like
I'm (not) keen on
I (don't) enjoy
I get bored with

shopping.
window-shopping.
visiting museums and art galleries.
visiting historical places.
being in the countryside.
swimming and sunbathing.
going for walks.
meeting people.
eating and drinking.
collecting stamps, postcards etc.
cooking at home.
watching television.

7 Using words and phrases from the exercises above, describe how you spend (a) your free time when you don't go away and (b) your holidays.

Illness and the Doctor

1 Match each of the following words with the correct item in the picture.

doctor   **patient**   **nurse**   **receptionist**   **lungs**
brain   **stomach**   **heart**   **chemist**

OPEN 9am–9pm

(a)

(b)   (c)

(d)

DOCTOR'S SURGERY

(e)

(f)

(g)
(h)

(i)

2 Put each of the following words or phrases in the correct space in the passage below.

look after   **treat**   **ache**   **examine**
suffer   **keep**   **cure**   **operate**

I am a family doctor. I have a nurse to help me and a receptionist to help the patients when they come to see me. When I see patients in my surgery, first I listen to their problems, then I (a) _____ them. Then, if I can, I (b) _____ them for their illnesses. Some simply have sore throats, headaches or flu and I give them a prescription to take to the chemist. Others (c) _____ from serious diseases of the heart, lungs, stomach or even brain. I can't always (d) _____ them myself and sometimes I have to send them to hospital for treatment. If something is seriously wrong with them, the hospital will decide to (e) _____ on them. The trouble is people don't (f) _____ themselves properly. It really isn't so difficult to (g) _____ well. If your head begins to (h) _____ , have a rest. If you always feel tired, get more exercise. Eat well. Have a good diet. And have a regular check-up with the doctor.

3 Put the correct word from the following list in each space below.

    for   **on**   **in**   **with**   **to**

(a) I saw the doctor _____ her surgery.
(b) She listened _____ my problems.
(c) They treated me _____ a heart problem.
(d) I took the prescription _____ the chemist.
(e) I had to go _____ hospital for an operation.
(f) Something's wrong _____ my back, doctor.
(g) They operated _____ him immediately.

4 For each sentence on the left below, find the correct meaning on the right.

(a) She got a hearing-aid.	(1)	She couldn't see things far away.
(b) She had no appetite.	(2)	Her head hurt.
(c) She was a bit deaf.	(3)	She didn't want to eat anything.
(d) She was short-sighted.	(4)	She bought something to help her hear better.
(e) She went on a diet.	(5)	She rested.
(f) She had a headache.	(6)	She couldn't hear very clearly.
(g) She cut down on cigarettes.	(7)	She decided to eat and drink only certain things.
(h) She took it easy.	(8)	She smoked less.

5 What advice would you give to a friend with the problems on the left? For each one, choose one *or more* items from the right.

(a) I've cut my finger badly.	(1)	Go and see a doctor.
(b) I think I've broken my leg.	(2)	Take a day or two off work.
(c) I'm always tired.	(3)	You'll probably need an X-ray.
(d) I'm smoking too much.	(4)	Why don't you have your eyes tested?
(e) I've got flu.	(5)	You should go on a diet.
(f) I'm getting a bit short-sighted.	(6)	The chemist will be able to give you something for it.
(g) I'm going deaf.	(7)	Well, you'd better cut down.
(h) I'm getting fat.	(8)	You might need a hearing-aid.
(i) There's something wrong with my heart.	(9)	Just take it easy for a few days.
(j) I'm drinking too much.	(10)	Go to bed for a few days.
(k) I've lost my appetite.	(11)	You should see a specialist.
(l) I've got a headache.	(12)	You need more exercise.
(m) I'm sleeping badly.	(13)	You may need an operation.

6 Describe your own health and any health problems you have.

In the Morning

1 Match each of the following words with the correct picture.

briefcase   shower   toothbrush   soap   teeth   hairbrush
newspaper   shaver   alarm clock   comb   clothes   pyjamas

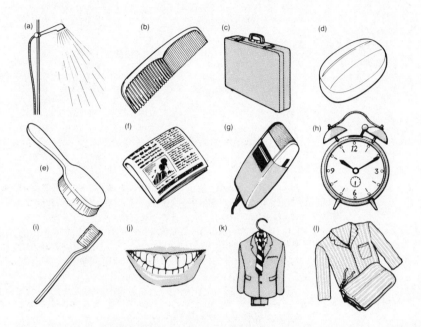

2 The following sentences are what people usually do in the morning. Put them in the right order, i.e. what we do first, what we do next, what we do after that, etc.

(a) I go into the bathroom.
(b) I turn off my alarm-clock.
(c) I get up.
(d) I sleep very heavily.
(e) I dress.
(f) My alarm clock goes off.
(g) I go into the kitchen.
(h) I wake up.
(i) I have my breakfast.
(j) I lie in bed for another ten minutes.
(k) I brush my teeth and comb my hair.
(l) I buy a newspaper.
(m) I catch a bus to work.
(n) I make my breakfast.
(o) I take my briefcase.
(p) I leave the house.
(q) I make my bed.
(r) I have a shower.

3

He's dressing

He's putting on his shirt

He's wearing a suit

Put the correct verb from the following list in each sentence below.

dress   **put on**   **wear**

(a) Policemen _____ uniforms so everyone knows who they are.
(b) It's cold. I think I'll _____ a pullover before I go out.
(c) I always _____ very quickly in the morning.
(d) William is only a baby. His mother has to _____ his shoes for him.
(e) At a wedding, people usually _____ their best clothes.
(f) After I get out of the swimming pool, I dry myself, _____ and go home.

4 Describe how you get up (a) on weekdays (working days) and (b) at weekends and on holiday.

The Telephone

1 Match each verb with the correct phrase below.

(a) dial (b) dial direct (c) look up (d) hold on (e) ring

(1) wait. (2) ring a phone number. (3) phone a number yourself without using the operator. (4) phone, call. (5) find information in a book.

2 Match each word or phrase on the left below with the correct phrase on the right.

(a)	wrong number	(1)	busy (when someone is using the line you want)
(b)	directory	(2)	public phone box
(c)	directory enquiries	(3)	person who helps you make a phone call
(d)	off-peak	(4)	phone number you get by mistake
(e)	interference	(5)	service you phone if you want to find a phone number
(f)	engaged	(6)	book of phone numbers
(g)	long-distance	(7)	very far, opposite of 'local'
(h)	call-box	(8)	not so busy time (when phone calls are cheaper)
(i)	operator	(9)	bad sound which makes it difficult to hear
(j)	receiver	(10)	prices, charges
(k)	rates	(11)	part of the phone you speak into and listen to

3 Put each of the words on the left in the exercise above in the correct space in the conversation below.

Bill: Is that Jane?
Nell: This is 377 0211. There's no one called Joan here.
Bill: Sorry, I must have the (a) _____ . Oh, just a moment. I want *Jane*, not Joan.
Nell: Oh sorry, yes. She's here. Hold on a moment.
Jane: Hello, this is Jane.
Bill: Hi, this is Bill. I tried to ring before, but the line was (b) _____ .
Jane: Yes, I was talking to my mother in Australia.
Bill: Oh, a (c) _____ call. Was it expensive? The (d) _____ are very high, aren't they?
Jane: Only if you go through the (e) _____ . It's quite cheap if you dial direct, especially if you phone during the (f) _____ period.
Bill: Was it a good line? Was it easy to hear?
Jane: It usually is, but today there was a lot of (g) _____ .
Bill: I need some help, Jane. I tried to look up Amy's number in the (h) _____ but I couldn't find it.
Jane: I'm afraid I haven't got it. Why don't you call (i) _____ ?
Bill: I'm in the street, in a (j) _____ , and I've got no more money.
Jane: But it's free. You just pick up the (k) _____ , then you dial 142.
Bill: Oh yes, how stupid!

Watching Television

1 What do you usually see on different television programmes? Match each type of programme on the left below with the correct item on the right.

(a) nature films
(b) quiz shows
(c) news and current affairs
(d) soap operas
(e) commercials

(f) travel films

(g) comedies
(h) sport
(i) educational programmes

(1) football, boxing, swimming etc.
(2) life in different countries
(3) people trying to win prizes by answering questions
(4) advertisements for products
(5) animals, fish, birds, flowers, plants etc.
(6) information about what's happening in the world
(7) jokes and funny situations
(8) information for pupils and students
(9) story of the daily life of a family

2 Which of the programmes above do you like? Use the following words.

relaxing   exciting   amusing   interesting   useful   boring

E.g. I find nature films interesting.

3 Put the correct word or phrase from the following list into the sentences below.

turn on   look up   plan   record   turn off   switch

(a) I _____ a programme if I don't like it.
(b) I _____ good programmes on my video-recorder.
(c) I _____ the television as soon as I get home.
(d) I _____ to another channel if I'm bored.
(e) I _____ my viewing very carefully.
(f) I _____ the times of the programmes in the newspaper.

4 Answer the following questions.

(a) What are your favourite types of programme?
(b) How do you watch television? (Do you plan carefully, record, watch everything?)
(c) How many hours television do you watch every day?
(d) What would you do without television?
(e) Is television good in your country?
(f) How many channels have you got in your country?
(g) What are the advantages and disadvantages of television?

HOW TO DO THINGS

How to Do the Washing Up

1 Match each of the following words with the correct item in the picture.

dishes   brush   cupboard   sink   washing-up liquid
sponge   cloth   drawer   tap   draining-board

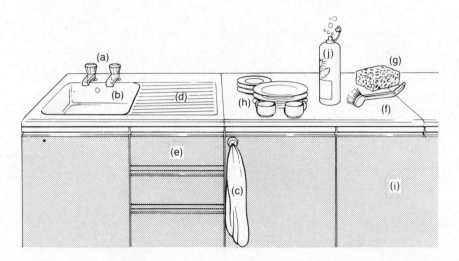

2 Put each of the following verbs in the correct space in the instructions below.

dry   rinse   turn off   fill
add   drain   put away   turn on

1 First put all the dirty dishes in the sink.
2 _____ the tap and _____ the sink with warm water. Then _____ the tap.
3 Now _____ some washing-up liquid.
4 Wash everything in the soapy water with a special sponge or brush.
5 _____ everything in clean water.
6 Put everything on the draining-board to _____ for a few minutes.
7 Then _____ everything with a cloth.
8 Finally _____ all the clean, dry things in cupboards or drawers.

3 Do you wash the dishes like this or differently? Describe how *you* wash the dishes.

How to Make an English Breakfast

1   Match each of the following words or phrases with the correct picture below.

bowl   jug   tea-bag   frying-pan   kettle   toaster
salt   pepper   teapot   table-cloth   napkin   glass

(a)   (b)   (c)   (d)

(e)   (f)   (g)   (h)

(i)   (j)   (k)   (l)

2   Put each of the following verbs in the correct space in the instructions below.

fry   boil   stir   clear away
add   pour   lay   spread

1 _____ the table (with the table-cloth, knives, forks, spoons, plates, glasses, napkins etc.)
2 To make tea, first _____ the water in a kettle.
3 Put a tea-bag in a cup and _____ the boiling water on it. (This is quicker than using a teapot.)
4 _____ milk (from a jug) and sugar (from a bowl), and _____ with a spoon.
5 Make some toast, using the toaster, and _____ butter on it.
6 _____ eggs and bacon in a frying-pan.
7 Put it on a plate with the toast, and eat it with a little salt and pepper.
8 When you've finished your breakfast, _____ all the breakfast things.

How to Do Keep-Fit Exercises

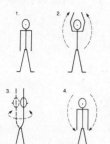

1 Put each of the following verbs in the correct space in the instructions below.

move   **raise**   **lower**   **turn**   **hang**   **stand**

1 _____ with your feet apart. Let your arms _____ by your sides.
2 _____ your arms above your head.
3 _____ your body first to the left, then to the right. (Don't _____ your feet.)
4 _____ your arms to your sides again.

2 Instructions as above.

touch   **lean**   **hold**   **bend**   **bring**   **straighten**

1 Sit on the front part of a chair, with your feet on the floor.
2 _____ the sides of the chair.
3 _____ back against the back of the chair.
4 _____ your knees, and _____ them up to _____ your chest.
5 _____ your legs and lower them to the floor again.

3 Using words from the exercises above, give instructions how to do these exercises.

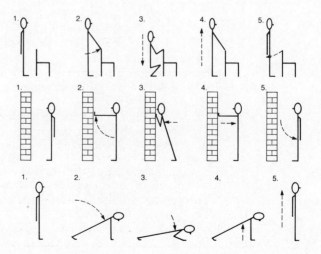

How to Use a Cassette Player

1 Match each of the following words with the correct item in the picture.

plug	**button**	**batteries**	**point**
knob	**switch**	**controls**	**lead**

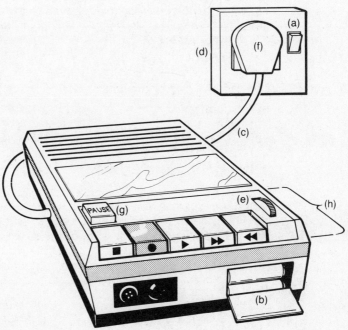

2 Put each of the following verbs in the correct space in the instructions below.

turn up	**press**	**unplug**	**switch on**
turn down	**turn**	**plug in**	**switch off**

1 First _____ at the nearest point.
2 Next _____ at the point.
  (The above will not be necessary if your machine is battery-operated)
3 Put a cassette in the machine and _____ the 'start' button.
4 To _____ the sound if it is too loud, _____ the 'volume' knob.
5 To _____ the sound if it is too low, turn the knob the other way.
6 You can adjust the quality of the sound by using the other controls.
7 When you have finished listening, press the 'stop' button.
8 Next _____ at the point.
9 Finally, _____ the machine.

RELATED WORD GROUPS

Basic Adjectives

In the exercises below finish each sentence on the left with the best phrase on the right.

1

(a)	Glue is	(1)	thin and straight.
(b)	Jam is	(2)	fragile and thin.
(c)	A wine-glass is	(3)	sweet and sticky.
(d)	A pin is	(4)	straight and sharp.
(e)	A ruler is	(5)	sticky and useful.

2

(a)	A hammer is	(1)	soft and cold.
(b)	Snow is	(2)	round and sweet.
(c)	A pullover is	(3)	hard and heavy.
(d)	A cigarette is	(4)	soft and warm.
(e)	An apple is	(5)	long and round.

3

(a)	An elephant is	(1)	expensive and powerful.
(b)	The Atlantic Ocean is	(2)	accurate and expensive.
(c)	A Rolex watch is	(3)	smooth and fragile.
(d)	A Rolls Royce car is	(4)	powerful and slow.
(e)	A mirror is	(5)	huge and deep

4

(a)	A comb is	(1)	round and hot.
(b)	The United States is	(2)	high and dangerous.
(c)	Mount Everest is	(3)	casual and useful.
(d)	Jeans are	(4)	wealthy and powerful.
(e)	The sun is	(5)	cheap and light.

5

(a)	A new baby is	(1)	hot and dry.
(b)	Fire is	(2)	rough and dangerous.
(c)	The Sahara Desert is	(3)	tiny and weak.
(d)	A stormy sea is	(4)	calm and smooth.
(e)	A quiet sea is	(5)	hot and dangerous.

6

(a)	A newspaper is	(1)	high and famous.
(b)	The Eiffel Tower is	(2)	rectangular and useful.
(c)	A motorway is	(3)	strong and dangerous.
(d)	A ball-point pen is	(4)	long and wide.
(e)	A tiger is	(5)	useful and cheap.

7 Use the above adjectives to describe each of the following.

(a) a cup	(f) a gun	(k) a millionaire	(p) a Sony Walkman
(b) a horse	(g) a passport	(l) a button	(q) a knife
(c) a cat	(h) an orange	(m) a Boeing 747	(r) a plate
(d) a bottle	(i) a pencil	(n) a sofa	(s) a space rocket
(e) chocolate	(j) ice cream	(o) sugar	(t) an overcoat

Basic Adjectives: opposites

In the exercises below replace each adjective with its opposite from the list above.

1 **thick**   **fat**   **deep**   **hot**   **good**   **late**

(a) It was a *bad* idea.
(b) He's very *thin*.
(c) The paper is *thin*.
(d) I took an *early* train.
(e) The water's very *shallow*.
(f) We had a *cold* meal.

2 **casual**   **dark**   **heavy**   **major**   **new**   **young**

(a) My luggage is *light*.
(b) It was a *light* evening.
(c) He's an *old* man.
(d) She wore *formal* clothes.
(e) It's a *minor* problem.
(f) It's an *old* book.

3 **wide**   **wealthy**   **smooth**   **busy**   **calm**   **small**

(a) It's a *big* room.
(b) What a *narrow* street!
(c) I've had a *quiet* day.
(d) They are a *poor* family.
(e) The wood was very *rough*.
(f) She felt *nervous* about her exam.

4 **safe**   **short**   **blunt**   **public**   **wonderful**   **clean**

(a) The knife's very *sharp*.
(b) It's a *dangerous* place.
(c) It was a *private* meeting.
(d) It was *terrible* news.
(e) He was wearing *dirty* clothes.
(f) The film was very *long*.

5 **huge**   **easy**   **low**   **guilty**   **empty**   **tight**

(a) The bottle is *full*.
(b) I am *innocent*.
(c) What a *difficult* question!
(d) It was a *tiny* animal.
(e) My belt is too *loose*.
(f) They are *high* buildings.

6 **dry**   **cheap**   **weak**   **wrong**   **nice**   **slow**

(a) It's a *fast* train.
(b) The weather was *nasty*.
(c) It was an *expensive* book.
(d) He gave the *right* answer.
(e) She's a *strong* woman.
(f) It was very *wet* weather.

7 **soft**   **ugly**   **rude**   **stupid**   **sad**   **quiet**

(a) He's an *intelligent* man.
(b) She feels very *happy*.
(c) He's a very *polite* boy.
(d) The chair was *hard*.
(e) They're *beautiful* buildings.
(f) The music was too *loud*.

Verbs

In each group below complete each sentence on the left with the
correct phrase on the right.

1

(a) We climb   (1) pictures and maps.
(b) We draw   (2) eggs to make an omelette.
(c) We weigh   (3) songs.
(d) We sing   (4) mountains, stairs and ladders.
(e) We break   (5) ourselves, or a parcel before we send it.

2

(a) We build   (1) people if we make a noise.
(b) We celebrate   (2) our jackets or seat-belts.
(c) We compare   (3) a birthday or success by having a party.
(d) We disturb   (4) houses or walls.
(e) We fasten   (5) two or more things to see which is better, cheaper etc.

3

(a) We feed   (1) a picture on the wall or our jacket on a peg.
(b) We fold   (2) a person's age if we don't know it.
(c) We guess   (3) hungry animals and children.
(d) We hang   (4) a football with our feet.
(e) We kick   (5) our clothes when we pack, or a map when we've finished using it.

4

(a) We knock   (1) a cigarette, a candle or a fire.
(b) We light   (2) a nail into the wall with a hammer.
(c) We mend   (3) bicycles, motor-bikes or horses.
(d) We punish   (4) clothes which are torn or have holes in them.
(e) We ride   (5) people who do wrong by sending them to prison.

5

(a) We repair   (1) a problem if we can.
(b) We rub   (2) food and drink to see if it's good.
(c) We shake   (3) broken machines, old cars and parts of a house.
(d) We solve   (4) a bottle of medicine before we drink it.
(e) We taste   (5) our hands if it's very cold.

Action Verbs

1 Match each of the following words with the correct picture.

hairdresser   **artist**   **driver**   **athlete**   **dressmaker**   **cleaner**

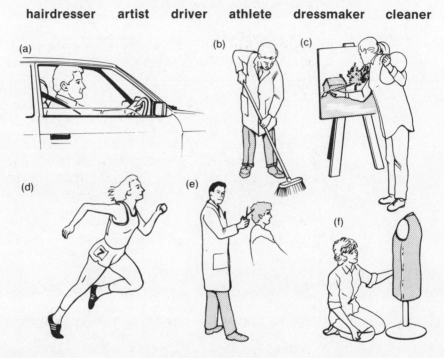

Which of them do the following things?

(g) cut, shampoo and comb
(h) dust, sweep and polish
(i) run, jump and throw

(j) measure, cut and sew
(k) draw, paint and sculpt
(l) accelerate, overtake and reverse

2 Instructions as above.

pilot   **teacher**   **dentist**   **postman**   **soldier**   **gardener**

(g) prepare, teach and mark
(h) collect, sort and deliver
(i) march, shoot and fight

(j) dig, plant and water
(k) take off, fly and land
(l) drill, fill and extract

Adjectives Describing Character

In each sentence below put the correct adjective from the group of three above it.

1   **impatient**   **sociable**   **adventurous**

(a) She loves meeting people and going to parties. She's a very _____ person.

(b) She likes new things and new places, even if they're difficult or dangerous. She's _____ .

(c) He gets very annoyed if he has to wait for anything. He doesn't like waiting. He's very _____ .

2   **ambitious**   **easy-going**   **talkative**

(a) He never gets upset or annoyed when things go wrong. He's a very _____ man.

(b) He loves to talk to people and tell them what he thinks and what he's done. He's _____ .

(c) She wants to get an important job in a high position. She's _____ .

3   **lazy**   **naughty**   **cheerful**

(a) Little Rosie is always breaking things and doing what her mother tells her *not* to do. She's a _____ girl.

(b) He doesn't like work. He prefers to do nothing. He's _____ .

(c) He's always happy and smiling. He's very _____ .

4   **sensible**   **selfish**   **optimistic**

(a) She only thinks about herself. She doesn't care about other people. She's _____ .

(b) He has a lot of common sense. He always knows the correct thing to do. He's a _____ boy.

(c) He always has good hopes for the future. He thinks everything will be fine. He's very _____ .

5   **polite**   **imaginative**   **tidy**

(a) She's very careful about her appearance and how she arranges her desk and her room. She's a _____ young lady.

(b) He always remembers to say 'please' and 'thank you'. He's very _____ .

(c) He has ideas like no-one else's. He can write wonderful stories, draw unusual pictures and suggest unusual ideas. He's extremely _____ .

6 For each of the 15 adjectives above find in the list below the best adjective which describes the *opposite* kind of person.

(a) impolite	(f) sad	(k) bad-tempered
(b) hard-working	(g) well-behaved	(l) unambitious
(c) silly	(h) patient	(m) cautious
(d) pessimistic	(i) quiet	(n) unselfish
(e) unsociable	(j) untidy	(o) unimaginative

People's Appearance

1 In each space (a) in the two descriptions of people below put the correct word from the following pair (a). Then do the same for (b), (c) etc.

(a) short
   strongly-built

(b) in his thirties
   elderly

(c) straight
   bald

(d) glasses
   bracelet

(e) his arms folded
   his hands on his hips

(f) casually-dressed
   formally-dressed

(g) checked
   striped

(h) well-pressed
   patched

(i) well-polished shoes
   trainers

He's a (a) _____ , (b) _____ man. He's about 75 and he's (c) _____ .
He's wearing (d) _____ and he's standing with (e) _____ . He's
(f) _____ in a dark suit and a (g) _____ shirt. His trousers are
(h) _____ and he's wearing (i) _____ .

He's a (a) _____ man. He's probably (b) _____ , maybe 34 or 35. He
has dark, (c) _____ hair. He has a (d) _____ on his wrist and he's
standing with (e) _____ . He's (f) _____ in a (g) _____ shirt and
(h) _____ jeans. He's wearing (i) _____ .

2 Instructions as Exercise 1.

(a) average height   (d) bow   (g) plain
    slim   necklace   spotted

(b) middle-aged   (e) her hands by her sides   (h) smart
    teenage   her hands clasped   baggy

(c) wavy   (f) untidily-dressed   (i) high-heeled shoes
    curly   neatly-dressed   sandals

She's a (a) _____ , (b) _____ woman of about 50. She has long,

(c) _____ hair. She's wearing a (d) _____ and she has (e) _____

in front of her. She is (f) _____ in a black and white (g) _____

blouse and a (h) _____ skirt. She's wearing black (i) _____ .

She's a (a) _____ . She's a (b) _____ girl of, perhaps, 18. She has

fair, (c) _____ hair with a (d) _____ in it. She has (e) _____ .

She's (f) _____ . She's wearing a dirty, (g) _____ tee-shirt, old,

(h) _____ trousers and a pair of (i) _____ .

3 Using the words and phrases from the above exercises, describe the
people below.

Materials

1 Complete each sentence below, using the correct material from the following list.

metal	**plastic**	**brick**	**wood**	**paper**
denim	**china**	**wool**	**stone**	**iron**
steel	**cotton**	**glass**	**leather**	**rubber**

(a) Pullovers are made of _____ .

(b) A mirror is made of _____ .

(c) Books are made of _____ .

(d) Underwear (vests, pants) is often made of _____ .

(e) Jeans, and often jackets and skirts, are made of _____ .

(f) The Pyramids of Egypt are made of _____ .

(g) Shoes are usually made of _____ .

(h) Coins are made of _____ .

(i) Houses in Britain are often made of _____ .

(j) A cheap ruler is made of _____ .

(k) Doors are usually made of _____ .

(l) The Eiffel Tower in Paris is made of _____ .

(m) Cutlery (knives, forks, spoons) is made of _____ .

(n) Crockery (plates, cups, saucers) is made of _____ .

(o) Car tyres are made of _____ .

2 What are the following things made of?

Cups, bottles, magazines, a watch, luggage, windows, envelopes, tables, a camera, jackets, typewriters, railway lines, Tower Bridge.

Geographical Words

1 Finish each sentence on the left with the correct phrase on the right.

(a) Africa is	(1) a city
(b) Canada is	(2) a river
(c) Manchester is	(3) a mountain
(d) London is	(4) a continent
(e) Sicily is	(5) a capital city
(f) The Amazon is	(6) a canal
(g) Everest is	(7) an ocean
(h) The Himalayas are	(8) a country
(i) The Atlantic is	(9) an island
(j) The Mediterranean is	(10) a desert
(k) The waterway across Panama between oceans is	(11) a mountain range
(l) The Sahara is	(12) a sea

2 What are the following?

Holland, Bali, the Nile, Kilimanjaro, the Caribbean, Liverpool, Paris, the Andes, Suez, Europe, the Gobi, Malaysia, New York, Fuji, Cairo, Cyprus, Asia, the Mississippi, the Pacific, the Thames, Brazil.

WORD BUILDING

'ful' and 'less'

It is sometimes (but *not always*) possible to make adjectives from nouns by putting 'ful' or 'less' on the end, e.g. 'careful' means '*with* care', 'careless' means '*without* care'.

Make a suitable adjective from the noun at the end of each sentence below by adding 'ful' or 'less' to the end.

(a) Thank you for the books. They will be very _____ for my studies. (use)

(b) This pen won't write at all. It's completely _____ (use)

(c) Thanks to modern technology, a visit to the dentist is now often quite _____. (pain)

(d) The policeman held my arms tightly behind my back. It was very _____. (pain)

(e) The government is trying to help _____ families. (home)

(f) Thank you for all you've done. You've been very _____. (help)

(g) I'm very, very tired. I had a _____ night last night. (sleep)

(h) We are _____ that the missing child will soon be found. (hope)

(i) What is this food? It has no taste. It's _____ (taste)

'Interesting' and 'Interested' etc.

The '*ing* form' of verbs, e.g. 'interesting', 'tiring', and the past participle, e.g. 'interested', 'tired', are often used as adjectives. The difference in meaning is seen in these sentences.

History was very *interesting* at school. I was very *interested* in it.

The journey was very *tiring*. We were very *tired* when we arrived.

Make the correct adjective, '*ing* form' or past participle, from the verb at the end of each sentence.

(a) It was a very _____ football match. (excite)

(b) The children were very _____ on Christmas day. (excite)

(c) We felt very _____ on holiday. (relax)

(d) It was a wonderfully _____ holiday. (relax)

(e) A shopkeeper likes to have _____ customers. (satisfy)

(f) She was a nurse and found it a very _____ job. (satisfy)

(g) It was a _____ film. I nearly fell asleep. (bore)

(h) The book was very badly written. I soon got _____ with it. (bore)

(i) After the explosion, the _____ children were taken to a safe place. (frighten)

(j) A _____ noise woke me up in the middle of the night. (frighten)

(k) He has an _____ habit of not looking at you when he's talking to you. (annoy)

(l) We've had lots of complaints from _____ customers about our bad service. (annoy)

'er' and 'or'

From an action verb we can sometimes make a noun ending 'er' or 'or' to describe the person who does the action, e.g. a 'player' is someone who plays (football, etc.), a 'conductor' is someone who conducts (an orchestra).

Make nouns ending 'er' or 'or' from these verbs.

(a) work er
(b) visit or
(c) clean er
(d) act or
(e) drive r
(f) employ er
(g) manage r
(h) direct or
(i) operate r
(j) make r
(k) paint er
(l) build er
(m) collect or
(n) sail or
(o) speak er

(Note: sometimes there is a small change in spelling, e.g. swim-swimmer, law-lawyer, empire-emperor, and a small number of nouns end in 'ar', e.g. lie-liar, beg-beggar)

'ist' and 'an'

From a noun we can sometimes make another noun ending 'ist' or 'an' to describe a person connected with the noun, e.g. a 'tobacconist' is someone who sells tobacco, a 'Brazilian' is someone from Brazil.

From these nouns make other nouns ending 'ist' or 'an' describing people. (Note: there are sometimes small changes in spelling.)

(a) Christ
(b) typewriter
(c) politics
(d) America
(e) piano
(f) science
(g) electricity
(h) bicycle
(i) art
(j) guitar
(k) Rome
(l) novel

'Hourly', 'Daily' etc.

We can make adjectives from 'hour', 'day', 'week', 'fortnight' (two weeks), 'month' and 'year' by adding 'ly' to the end. Put each of the following words in its correct place in the sentences below.

hourly   daily   weekly   fortnightly   monthly   yearly

(a) The most famous British _____ newspaper is *The Times*.
(b) *Time* is an American _____ news magazine. I buy it every Tuesday.
(c) Her salary is £12,000 a year and she receives a _____ increase every September.
(d) He could possibly die in 24 hours. The doctors are giving him _____ tests to check his condition.
(e) She goes to see her parents every two weeks. They always look forward to these _____ visits.
(f) I haven't yet received my _____ salary cheque for February.

'en'

1 We can often make a verb from an adjective (or sometimes a noun, e.g. 'length', 'strength') by adding 'en' to the end. 'To darken' means 'to make dark' or 'to become dark'.

E.g. He darkened his hair to change his appearance.
The sky darkened as the clouds covered the sun.

In the spaces below put a verb ending 'en' made from the adjective or noun in brackets.

(a) Some screws in this machine are loose. I must _____ them. (tight)
(b) My belt is very tight and uncomfortable. I'll _____ it. (loose)
(c) Soon the dark clouds went away and the sky began to _____ . (bright)
(d) This pencil isn't very sharp. It's blunt. I'll _____ it. (sharp)
(e) This noise is so loud it'll _____ me. (deaf)
(f) The river is quite narrow here, but as it gets near the sea it begins to _____ . (wide)
(g) The runway is too short to take large, modern planes. They're going to _____ it. (length)
(h) The bridge is dangerous. It's not strong enough. There are plans to _____ it. (strength)

Number + Noun

Instead of saying 'a journey which took three hours', we can say 'a *three-hour* journey'. We have made a compound adjective by connecting the number and the noun, *which is used in the singular.* In the spaces below put similar compound adjectives made from the words in italics in the brackets.

E.g. He was wearing a _____ suit. (It cost *500 dollars*)
He was wearing a *500-dollar* suit.

(a) We went on a _____ walk. (We went *five miles*)
(b) There will now be a _____ break. (It will last *ten minutes*)
(c) She's written a _____ book. (It has *200 pages*)
(d) It's a _____ hotel. (It has *20 storeys*)
(e) We had a _____ holiday. (It lasted *two weeks*)
(f) He's bought a _____ boat. (It's *ten metres* long)
(g) She's started a _____ English course. (It will last *six months*)
(h) The President will go on a _____ tour in April. (He'll visit *five countries*)
(i) He drives a _____ lorry. (It weighs *two tons*)

'un', 'dis', 'in', 'im', 'il', 'ir'

1 To give some words an opposite meaning, 'un' is put in front of them, e.g. She was very *unhappy.* Put 'un' in front of the following words and then put each word in its correct space below.

necessary   healthy   well   punctual   employed   fair   pleasant

Vera: You look rather (a) _____ . Why don't you see a doctor?

Alan: Oh no, that's (b) _____ . I've just been working hard. I'm writing a book.

Vera: In this room? With the windows closed? And you smoke. That's very (c) _____ . You'll be ill.

Alan: But if I open the windows, some very (d) _____ smells come in from the chemical factory.

Vera: And I hear you've been (e) _____ since you lost your job in the library.

Alan: Yes, they said I was (f) _____ . But in fact I was only late a few times. It was very (g) _____ .

2 Instructions as above.

satisfactory   friendly   conscious   usual   hurt   tidy   successful

(a) Just look at your room. It looks awful. It's so _____ .

(b) He doesn't like the children in his new school. They're rather _____ .

(c) I'm afraid your work is _____ . You'll have to do better.

(d) It was an _____ film. I've never seen one like it.

(e) He hit his head on the door as he fell and was _____ for 20 minutes.

(f) I applied for the job but I was _____ .

(g) Two people were injured in the accident but fortunately everyone else was _____ .

3 Instructions as above.

dress   wrap   tie   lock   do   pack

I like going away for a holiday but the best part is coming home again. I arrive home. I (a) _____ the door of my flat. I put my suitcase on the floor and start to (b) _____ it. I take out the things I have bought on holiday. I (c) _____ the string. I carefully (d) _____ them, look at them and put them on the table. I feel tired but very happy. I go into the bedroom. I (e) _____ my jacket and shoes. I take them off. I (f) _____ and I have a bath. I relax. I'm home again.

4 Put each of the following words in the correct space below. The words will be made opposite in meaning by the 'dis', 'in', 'im', 'il' or 'ir' already in the sentence.

convenient   polite   formal   honest   regular   correct   legal

(a) I'm afraid the buses here are very ir _____ . I sometimes have to wait an hour.
(b) This information is in _____ . The train leaves at 3.10, not 3.20.
(c) The use of certain dangerous drugs is il _____ . It's against the law.
(d) His house isn't near the shops, transport or his work. It's in a very in _____ place.
(e) She didn't say 'please' or 'thank you'. She was very im _____ .
(f) It's not a special occasion. Just wear ordinary, in _____ clothes.
(g) She steals. She tells lies. She's completely dis _____ .

Adverbs of Manner

Adverbs of manner tell us *how* something is done, e.g. She sings *beautifully*. They also describe adjectives, e.g. She was *extremely successful*.

They are usually made from adjectives and usually end in 'ly':
slow–slowly; careful–carefully; dangerous–dangerously

Adjectives ending in 'y' usually drop the 'y' and add 'ily' to make the adverb:
happy–happily; lazy–lazily; sleepy–sleepily

Adjectives ending in 'ic' usually add 'ally' to make the adverb (but note: 'public' 'publicly'):
tragic–tragically; comic–comically; basic–basically

Some adjectives do not change as adverbs:
fast–fast; hard–hard; daily–daily; late–late

In the following sentences put in each space the adverb made from the adjective in brackets.

(a) I'm afraid I _____ forgot to bring my camera. (stupid)
(b) It rained _____ for three hours. (continuous)
(c) He died _____ , trying to save his friend's life. (heroic)
(d) The children were playing _____ in the garden. (noisy)
(e) Please answer my questions _____ . (truthful)
(f) The film ended _____ with the hero's death in a gun-fight. (dramatic)
(g) She worked very _____ . (hard)
(h) He looked _____ at the person who had interrupted. (angry)
(i) She promised _____ that the government would not raise taxes. (public)
(j) He's usually very lively, but today he's _____ quiet. (strange)
(k) He arranged his desk very _____ , everything in its right place. (tidy)
(l) I agree with you _____ . You're _____ right. (complete, absolute)

Compound Nouns

The important thing to remember in a compound noun (i.e. two nouns put together) is that the second noun is the real noun. The first is used like an adjective to describe what kind of thing or person the second noun is, e.g. a bedroom is a room with a bed in it.

There is no simple rule to tell you when the two parts of a compound noun are written together, with a hyphen or separately. You must learn the written form every time you learn a new compound noun, e.g. policeman, shoe-shop, railway station.

1   Make compound nouns from the following phrases.

E.g. a pot to make tea in: a teapot

(a) a party for someone's birthday
(b) a mark used after a question
(c) a library of a college
(d) a student at university
(e) furniture used in an office
(f)   clothes we wear at work
(g) a driver of a lorry
(h) a programme on television
(i)   a building used by the government
(j)   a class held in the evening
(k) a window of a shop
(l)   a knife for cutting bread

In a compound noun the first noun is usually in the singular. Make compound nouns from the following phrases.

E.g. a seller of flowers: a flower-seller

(m) a book to write exercises in
(n) an inspector of tickets
(o) a brush to keep your teeth clean
(p) an album you stick stamps in
(q) a map which shows roads
(r) a lace used for tying shoes
(s) juice from oranges
(t)   a list of books
(u) a magazine about films
(v) a shop selling cameras
(w) a bus which carries tourists

2   When a compound noun is used in the plural, it is normally the second noun (the 'real' noun) which is made plural. The first one, like an adjective, remains singular. Make the following plural.

E.g. policeman – policemen; shoe-shop – shoe-shops; railway station – railway stations

(a) stamp collection
(b) city-centre
(c) teacup
(d) concert-hall
(e) family doctor
(f)   picture-frame
(g) dog owner
(h) car-wheel
(i)   airline pilot
(j)   matchbox

Word Forms

In each space in the exercises below put the correct word from the two or three above it.

1 decide (verb)   **decision** (noun)
Will you take the job? We must have a quick _____ . You must _____ very soon.

2 congratulate (verb)   **congratulations** (noun)
I'd like to _____ you on passing your exam. Many _____ !

3 permit (verb)   **permission** (noun)
We cannot _____ children under 14 to go without their parents' _____

4 invite (verb)   **invitation** (noun)
Did we send the Smiths an _____ to our party? Did we _____ them?

5 arrive (verb)   **arrival** (noun)
The _____ of the London train will be 15 minutes late. It will _____ at 10.45.

6 depart (verb)   **departure** (noun)
The next train for Newcastle will _____ from platform 4. The _____ will be in ten minutes.

7 complain (verb)   **complaint** (noun)
I think I'll _____ about this bad service. I'll make a _____ .

8 argue (verb)   **argument** (noun)
They don't get on well. They often _____ . They're having an _____ now.

9 importance (noun)   **important** (adjective)
It doesn't matter. It's of no _____ . It's not _____ .

10 difficulty (noun)   **difficult** (adjective)
It's very _____ to operate this machine. I have great _____ in doing it.

11 height (noun)   **high** (adjective)
What's the _____ of that mountain? How _____ is it?

12 arrange (verb)   **arrangement** (noun)
I don't like the _____ of the furniture in this room. I think I'll _____ it differently.

13 bleed (verb)   **blood** (noun)
If you don't do something about that cut, it'll _____ all over the place. There'll be _____ everywhere.

14 practise (verb)   **practice** (noun)
You need more English _____ . You must _____ more.

15 describe (verb)   **description** (noun)
I gave the police a _____ of the stolen goods. I had to _____
everything.

16 explain (verb)   **explanation** (noun)
I'd like an _____ of your absence. Please _____ why you weren't at
work yesterday.

17 enjoy (verb)   **enjoyable** (adjective)
I always have a good time at your parties. I always _____ them.
They're very _____ .

18 fly (verb)   **flight** (noun)
We _____ to Brazil on Thursday. Our _____ is at 10.45 a.m.

19 sign (verb)   **signature** (noun)
I need your _____ on this paper, please. Could you _____ here?

20 meet (verb)   **meeting** (noun)
I'm going to _____ some friends tomorrow. Our _____ is at two
o'clock.

21 heat (noun)   **hot** (adjective)
It's a very _____ country. The _____ is too much for me.

22 suit (verb)   **suitable** (adjective)
What about six o'clock? Will that time _____ you? Will that be a _____
time?

23 relax (verb)   **relaxation** (noun)
On holiday I don't like to do anything. I just want sun, sleep, food and
_____ . I just want to take it easy and _____ .

24 choose (verb)   **choice** (noun).
I don't know which one to _____ . It's difficult to make a _____ .

25 legalize (verb)   **legal** (adjective)
It isn't _____ to sell alcohol to children, and the government has no
plans to _____ it.

26 modernize (verb)   **modern** (adjective)
My kitchen is very old. I'm going to _____ it. I've always wanted a
_____ kitchen.

27 industry (noun)   **industrial** (adjective)
Japan's _____ has made her rich. Japan is an _____ country.

28 agriculture (noun)   **agricultural** (adjective)
This is an _____ area. There are no factories, only farms, only _____ .

29 simplify (verb)   **simple** (adjective)
This explanation is too complicated. Can you make it more _____ ?
Can you _____ it?

30 admit (verb)   **admission** (noun)
This ticket will _____ one person free. It will give free _____ .

31 freedom (noun)   **free** (adjective)
The people demonstrated for more _____ . They wanted to be _____ .

32 weigh (verb)   **weight** (noun)
I _____ 65 kilos. What's your _____ ?

33 noise (noun)   **noisy** (adjective)
It's very _____ here. Where's the _____ coming from?

34 safety (noun)   **safe** (adjective)
I'm worried about the children's _____ . I hope they're _____ .

35 danger (noun)   **dangerous** (adjective)
The children can play here. It's not _____ at all. There's no _____ .

36 peace (noun)   **peaceful** (adjective)
You'll find all the _____ you want here. It's a very quiet, _____ place.

37 lose (verb)   **loss** (noun)
If you _____ your money, you should tell the police about the _____ at once.

38 mix (verb)   **mixture** (noun)
First _____ everything together and then put the _____ in a saucepan.

39 dirt (noun)   **dirty** (adjective)
It was a very _____ place. There was _____ everywhere.

40 violence (noun)   **violent** (adjective)
We live in _____ times. There are pictures of _____ in the newspapers every day.

41 measure (verb)   **measurement** (noun)
How long is it? The _____ must be very exact. _____ it very carefully.

42 kindness (noun)   **kind** (adjective)
She was very _____ to us. I thanked her for her _____ .

43 happiness (noun)   **happy** (adjective)   **happily** (adverb)
(a) The children played _____ in the garden all morning.
(b) He has a good job and a lovely family. He's a very _____ man.
(c) Their children gave them a lot of _____ .

44 succeed (verb)   **success** (noun)   **successful** (adjective)
(a) The film was a great _____ . It made 75 million dollars.
(b) Do you think they will _____ in finishing the work this week?
(c) He was very _____ in his job and soon became Managing Director.

45 die (verb)   **death** (noun)   **dead** (adjective)
(a) If the doctor doesn't come soon, she'll _____ .
(b) The police found a _____ body in the river.
(c) The _____ of the President was announced on television.

IDIOMS

Verb Phrases

1 Put each of the following phrases in the correct space in the conversation below.

make an appointment   **make a noise**   **make sure**
make your breakfast   **make a list**   **make your bed**

Mother: George, don't forget to (a) _____ and tidy your room. It's nine o'clock. I'm going shopping.
George: OK, Mum. Can you buy some things for me, please?
Mother: Yes, (b) _____ of the things you want and give it to me. Quickly.
George: OK. I've got to (c) _____ with the dentist. I've got toothache.
Mother: Alright. I'm going out in two minutes. You'll have to (d) _____ yourself. There's plenty of bread and eggs and tea.
George: OK, Mum.
Mother: And (e) _____ you wash up afterwards! Don't forget.
George: Alright. Here's the list of things I want. Thanks.
Mother: Right. And don't (f) _____ in the kitchen. Keep quiet. Remember your father's in bed with flu.

2 Put each of the following phrases in the correct space in the passage below.

make a decision   **make friends**   **make enquiries**
make some money   **make plans**   **make an effort**

To go and live abroad or not? It needs a lot of thought. After you (a) _____ to go, you must organize yourself. First (b) _____ in your own country about accommodation, language schools and work possibilities. You'll need this information so that you can (c) _____ . In the new country, perhaps it will be the first time you've lived alone. Maybe you'll want to get a job to (d) _____ so you'll have to look for work. You might feel lonely and you'll have to (e) _____ with other young people. Sometimes this isn't easy in a big city. Well, it's up to you. You'll have to (f) _____ .

3 Put each of the following phrases in the correct space in the sentences below.

take an exam   **take a seat**   **take place**
take a photo   **take any notice**   **take care**

(a) This vase is very old and valuable. Please _____ when you clean it.
(b) Look at that lovely old house. I think I'll _____ of it.
(c) He's working very hard every evening. He's going to _____ next month.
(d) Mr Jenkins will be here in a moment. Please _____ .
(e) I told him it was a dangerous machine, but he didn't _____ . That's why he hurt his hand.
(f) The meeting will _____ in the director's office at 11 a.m.

4 Put each of the following phrases in the correct space in the conversation below.

have a rest   **have a party**   **have a game of tennis**
have a bath   **have fun**   **have breakfast**

Jennie: What do you do on Saturdays?
Donald: Well, I get up late and (a) _____ or shower.
Jennie: Then you (b) _____ ?
Donald: Yes, bacon and eggs. Fruit juice. Then I usually (c) _____ in the park with a friend.
Jennie: Oh, are you good at tennis?
Donald: No, but we enjoy ourselves. We (d) _____ .
Jennie: And in the evening?
Donald: Oh, I usually invite a few friends to my place and we (e) _____ . You know, music, food, drinks, dancing.
Jennie: And on Sunday?
Donald: On Sunday I don't do anything. I just (f) _____ .

5 Put each of the following phrases in the correct space in the sentences below.

keep calm   **keep still**   **keep awake**
keep fit   **keep quiet**   **keep a record**

(a) They _____ by walking, running and swimming every day.
(b) I want to draw a picture of you. Don't move. _____ .
(c) Ladies and gentlemen, there is a small fire in the cinema. There's no need to worry. Please just _____ and leave by the exit doors.
(d) Teachers must _____ of student attendance by filling in the class register every day.
(e) I'm so tired I don't think I can _____ any longer.
(f) The children are asleep so don't make a noise. _____ .

6 Put each of the following phrases in the correct space in the passage below.

do my shopping   **do me good**   **do a lot of harm**
do exercises   **do some work**   **do the housework**

I think I'm very well-organized. I (a) _____ at the supermarket every evening on my way home from work. When I get home, I (b) _____ (cleaning, washing, tidying up etc.). After dinner I (c) _____ I've brought home from the office. Before I go to bed, I (d) _____ to keep in good condition. I think they (e) _____ because I'm always fit and well. I don't smoke at all. I think cigarettes (f) _____ .

7 Put each of the following phrases in the correct space in the sentences below.

get a train   **get ready**   **get a lot of money**
get married   **get flu**

(a) Jim and Rosemarie are going to _____ and I'm going to the wedding.
(b) Nurses do a wonderful job but they don't _____ .
(c) If you don't put on more clothes in this cold weather, you'll _____ .
(d) The buses are very slow. Let's _____ .
(e) We're going out in five minutes, children. Hurry up. _____ . Put your coats on.

'Touch'

Put each of the following phrases in the correct space in the passage below.

get in touch   **keep in touch**   **get out of touch**

Well goodbye, Murray. I hope you have a good time in Africa. You've got my address, so please (a) _____ . Write sometimes. It would be a pity to (b) _____ . Oh, have you got Ann's address? I don't know where she is. I want to (c) _____ with her to ask her to a party.

Prepositional Phrases

1   Put each of the following phrases in the correct space in the passage below.

at school   **at work**   **at once**   **at least**
at the seaside   **at home**   **at last**   **at first**

I'll always remember that day. I was 15. I had a bad cold and I was (a) _____ alone. My father was (b) _____ (he's a bus-driver). My older sister had gone to the coast for a day (c) _____ . My 13-year-old brother was (d) _____ . My mother was out shopping. I heard a strange noise. (e) _____ I thought it was my mother returning, but it wasn't the door. It was water! Rain? No, it wasn't raining. The kitchen taps? No, they were off. The bathroom? No. I thought and thought. It must have been (f) _____ ten minutes before I realized the noise came from the flat upstairs. (g) _____ I ran upstairs and knocked on Mr Black's door. No answer. I knocked again. And again. (h) _____ he came and opened it. He had turned on the water for a bath, forgotten all about it and fallen asleep in his chair.

2   Put each of the following phrases in the correct space in the conversation below.

on foot   **on holiday**   **on the other hand**   **on fire**
on time   **on business**   **on second thoughts**   **on the one hand**

Pam: Hi, Sue. Am I late? The traffic was terrible.
Sue: No, you're not late. It's exactly six o'clock. You're exactly
       (a) _____ . What's the matter?
Pam: Firemen and fire-engines everywhere. There's a house (b) _____
       near the cinema. I couldn't get a bus. I had to come (c) _____ .
Sue: Well anyway, you're here. Liz can't come. She's in Italy.
Pam: Oh, is she (d) _____ ? Italy's lovely at this time of the year.
Sue: No, she had to go there (e) _____ . She's gone to a meeting for
       her firm.
Pam: Well, where shall we go for *our* holiday? Spain? I don't know.
       (f) _____ Spain's always sunny in summer, but (g) _____ it's a
       bit crowded.
Sue: Yes, I thought of Spain too, but (h) _____ I think I'd prefer
       Holland.

3 Put each of the following phrases in the correct space in the sentences below.

in prison	**in a hurry**	**in time**	**in trouble**
in love	**in person**	**in tears**	**in a mess**

(a) You can't make a reservation by phone or post. You must do it
 _____ .

(b) She rang the police and they arrived just _____ to catch the burglar.

(c) He spent six years _____ for the crime.

(d) Please tidy up your room. It looks awful. It's really _____ .

(e) He's very difficult to control. He's always _____ at school.

(f) Andrew's been very quiet recently. I think he's _____ with the new girl at the office.

(g) The children were very shocked and upset by the sad news. Many of them were _____ .

(h) Sorry I can't stop and talk now. I'm _____ .

4 Put each of the following phrases in the correct space in the conversation below.

by chance	**by all means**	**by bus**	**by post**
by phone	**by the way**	**by car**	**by mistake**

Jack: I've done something stupid. (a) _____ I told Sara I'd meet her tomorrow. I meant to say the day after tomorrow. Tomorrow I'm busy at the office.

Alex: Can't you contact her and explain?

Jack: That's the problem. A letter wouldn't reach her in time, so I can't let her know (b) _____ . How can I tell her?

Alex: (c) _____ , or don't you know her number?

Jack: She hasn't got a phone. Have you, (d) _____ , got her neighbours' number? You know. The Smiths.

Alex: No, sorry. Why don't you drive to her flat now? You could get there in an hour (e) _____ .

Jack: No, it's being repaired, and it would take ages to go (f) _____ . Anyway, she's miles from a bus-route. Alex, do you think you could phone her at her office tomorrow morning?

Alex: (g) _____ , of course. Good idea. (h) _____ , when will your car be OK again? I was going to ask if I could borrow it on Saturday.

5 Put each of the following phrases in the correct space in the sentences below.

out of doors	**out of control**	**out of date**
out of breath	**out of order**	**out of work**

(a) This timetable's no good. It's last year's. It's _____ .

(b) He's very sunburnt and healthy. He spends a lot of time _____ .

(c) This telephone doesn't work. It's _____ .

(d) If the government doesn't do something very quickly, the situation will get _____ .

(e) He'd been running hard and arrived _____ .

(f) He's been _____ for four months, but he thinks he'll get a job soon.

Pairs

1   Put each of the following phrases in the correct space in the sentences below.

more or less   **on and off**   **yes and no**   **so and so**

(a) I've _____ finished the book. I've got two more pages to read.
(b) In English, you begin a letter 'Dear _____'.
(c) I've been learning English for six years _____ . There were several breaks in that time, when I was too busy to study.
(d) Do I like my new job? Well, _____ . I'm not sure yet.

2   Instructions as above.

peace and quiet   **likes and dislikes**
do's and don'ts   **little by little**

(a) Uncle Henry's coming to stay this weekend. What does he like to eat? Where will he want to go? Has he any particular _____ ?
(b) At first I found the new job strange and difficult, but _____ I settled down.
(c) The school is quite a relaxed place. It's not strict at all. There aren't many _____ .
(d) What a noisy, busy job this is. I'm looking forward to getting some _____ in the country this weekend.

Time

Put each of the following phrases in the correct space in the conversation below.

one day   **from now on**   **ages**
for good   **the other day**   **so far**

Fiona: Hello, Sally. I haven't seen you for (a) _____ . At least a year. How are you?

Sally: Hi, Fiona. I'm fine. I've just started a new business. We started (b) _____ . In fact it was just last Thursday.

Fiona: Yes, I heard about it. And I've seen your shop. How's business?

Sally: Well, after only a few days I'm not sure. (c) _____ it's been good, but we sell swim-suits and the weather's been very sunny, but now it's turning cold so (d) _____ it might not be so good.

Fiona: What about you and Jimmy? Are you two married yet?

Sally: No, but probably in the future. I don't know when. (e) _____ . What about you? You've been abroad a lot. Are you going away again?

Fiona: No, I've had enough travelling. I'm staying here (f) _____ . Well, I've got to go. See you soon. I need a swim-suit.

'Mind'

Put each of the following phrases in the correct space in the conversation below.

change your mind   **I don't mind**   **mind your head**
make up your mind   **in two minds**

(a) Shall I go to America or not? I can't decide. I'm _____ about it.
(b) I'm depending on you to help me tomorrow. I hope you don't

     _____.

(c) You must decide soon. Come on, _____ .
(d) This door is very low so _____ .
(e) It doesn't matter if you come late. It's OK. _____ .

Things We Say

The exercises below give phrases often used in common situations. In each exercise find the best answer on the right to each phrase on the left.

1

(a) How do you do?   (1) Bye. See you.
(b) How are you?   (2) Many happy returns!
(c) It's my birthday.   (3) I'm fine.
(d) I'm off.   (4) How do you do?

2

(a) Hi!   (1) Congratulations!
(b) I've passed my exam!   (2) Oh, hard luck.
(c) I've failed my exam.   (3) He's around somewhere.
(d) Where's Jack?   (4) Hi!

3

(a) Thank you very much.   (1) I'd love to.
(b) I'm sorry I can't help you.   (2) Sorry, I've no idea.
(c) Where's the post-office, please?   (3) Never mind. Thanks anyway.
(d) Do you fancy coming to the cinema tonight?   (4) Not at all.

4

(a) What a nice flat you have.   (1) Wait and see.
(b) Are you hungry?   (2) Yes, make yourself at home.
(c) What are you going to give me for my birthday?   (3) Yes, I'm starving.
(d) Come on. We're late.   (4) Just a moment. Hang on.

MISCELLANEOUS

Abbreviations

1 Put each of the following abbreviations in the correct place in the note below, which Julie left for her flat-mate, Molly.

Abbreviation	Meaning	We say . . .
etc.	and so on (*et cetera*)	'and so on' *or* 'et cetera'
e.g.	for example (*exempli gratia*)	'for example' *or* 'for instance'
c/o	care of (in an address)	'care of'
a.m.	before noon (*ante meridiem*)	'a.m.'
p.m.	after noon (*post meridiem*)	'p.m.'
Rd	road (in an address)	'road'
PTO	Please Turn Over (at the bottom of a page)	'please turn over'
NB	note well, pay special attention (*nota bene*)	'NB'
PS	after writing (*postscript*)	'PS'
US	United States of America	'US'

10.30 (a) _am_ Friday
Molly,
I'm just going out to visit my mother. I'll be back this evening
(about 7 (b) _am_). No time to go shopping. Haven't got anything
for dinner tonight. Can you get bread, potatoes, beef,
tomatoes (c) ___ ? And get something to drink, (d) ___
wine. ((e) ___ Don't buy expensive stuff ! We can't
afford it !)

                       Julie

(f) ___ Someone phoned for you. I didn't know him.
Fred Somers.   Friend of yours just arrived from (g) ___
(I think he said Chicago).
His address: (h) ___ Mr & Mrs Watson, 14 York (i) ___,
London N.W.4.   He hasn't a phone.   He said
he'll phone again.   I suggested that he should
                                     (j) ___

2 Put each of the following abbreviations in the correct place in the passage below.

Abbreviation	Meaning	We say . . .
BC	Before Christ	'BC' or 'Before Christ'
AD	After Christ (*Anno*) *Domini*)	'AD' or 'After Christ'
i.e.	this means (*id est*)	'that is' or 'i.e.'
lb(s)	pound(s) weight (*libra*) (1 lb = 0.454 kg)	'pound(s)'
in(s) (")	inch(es) (1 in = 2.54 cm)	'inch(es)'
ft (')	foot/feet (1 ft = 0.3048 m)	'foot/feet'
UK	United Kingdom	'UK' or 'United Kingdom'
EEC	European Economic Community	'EEC'
USSR	Union of Soviet Socialist Republics	'USSR'

The piece of stone is about 1 (a) _____ 9 (b) _____ long and weighs nearly 6 (c) _____ . It bears the name of the Egyptian King Tutankhamen, who died over 3,000 years ago in 1343 (d) _____ . It was discovered almost exactly 3,000 years after his death in 1655 (e) _____ and taken to Constantinople ((f) _____ the modern Istanbul). It will shortly go on a tour of museums in France, Italy, Spain, West Germany and other (g) _____ countries, including, we hope, the (h) _____ . Next year it will be exhibited in Moscow, Leningrad and other cities in the (i) _____ .

3 Read the following sentences as they would normally be spoken.

(a) I work from 8.30 a.m. to 4 p.m. and do housework e.g. cleaning, washing etc.
(b) His address is c/o Mrs L. Steel, 4 Dover Rd, Chicago, US.
(c) At the bottom of his letter he writes, 'PS I'm going to Scotland next month,' then, 'PTO', then he continues, 'NB Please use my London address for letters.'
(d) The average height of a man in the UK is 5ft 8ins, i.e. about 173 centimetres.
(e) The USSR is having talks with EEC leaders.
(f) A metal object 1' 9" long of about 500 BC was found in the third century AD.

Reading Dates and Numbers

1 Write the following sentences as they would normally be written.

E.g. He paid one hundred and sixty pounds: He paid £160.

(a) He died on the sixth of April seventeen forty-three.
(b) They cost two pounds thirty-five pence.
(c) My phone number is three seven oh double-four nine two.
(d) There are one thousand two hundred and seventy-six people in the village.
(e) One centimetre is nought point three nine three seven inches.

2 Read the following sentences as they would normally be spoken.

(a) I was born on 4th May, 1937.
(b) The tickets were £4.50 each.
(c) Phone me on 408 9117.
(d) The price is £12,750.
(e) 1lb = 0.454 kilograms.

Punctuation Marks

Match each of the following words or phrases with the correct punctuation mark below.

apostrophe	**inverted commas**	**hyphen**	**comma**
small letter	**exclamation mark**	**question mark**	**full stop**
brackets	**capital letter**		

(a)

'Look out!' he shouted. (c)
(b)

'What's the matter?' she asked.
(d)

'There's a motor-bike,' he said.
(g)
(e) (f) (h) (i)

(continued on page 6)
(j)

Spelling: noun plurals

1

	Singular	Plural	Points
final *s, ss, ch, sh, x*	bus, boss, church, brush, box	buses, bosses, churches, brushes, boxes	add *es*
final *y*	boy, donkey, tray, valley	boys, donkeys, trays, valleys	add *s* if final *y* follows vowel (*a,e,i,o,u*)
	fly, lady, body, lorry	flies, ladies, bodies, lorries	drop *y* and add *ies* if *y* follows consonant
	sheep, fish	sheep, fish	no change in plural

Put the words in brackets into the correct plural forms.

(a) We send you our best (wish) and many (kiss).
(b) He bought a dozen (box) of (match).
(c) For Christmas he gave his sons (watch) and his daughters (dress).
(d) The (boy) are doing very well in their (study).
(e) She collects children's (toy) from different (country).
(f) (Library) are usually closed on (Sunday).
(g) (Family) of (monkey) have different (way) of looking after their (baby).
(h) He has 30 cows, 65 pigs and over 80 (sheep).
(i) I often go to the river to see the birds and the (fish).

2

	Singular	Plural	Points
final *f, fe*	knife, shelf, self, life, wife	knives, shelves, selves, lives, wives	many nouns drop *f, fe* and add *ves*
	roof, safe, handkerchief	roofs, safes, handkerchiefs	the others just add *s*
final *o*	tomato, potato, volcano, hero	tomatoes, potatoes, volcanoes, heroes	many nouns add *es*
	piano, photo, kilo	pianos, photos, kilos	the others just add *s*
irregular	child, tooth, man woman, foot	children, teeth, men, women, feet	

Put the words in brackets into the correct plural forms.

(a) Be careful, children. You'll hurt (yourself) with those sharp (knife).
(b) Their (wife) waved their (handkerchief) until the train had disappeared from view.
(c) Three people have recently lost their (life) falling from high (roof).
(d) He bought two (kilo) of (tomato).
(e) Here are some (photo) of famous (hero) of the Second World War.
(f) (Woman) can damage their (foot) by not wearing suitable shoes.
(g) (Child) should brush their (tooth) twice a day.

Spelling: verbs ending in 'y'

Verbs	3rd person singular, present simple tense	Regular 'ed' form	Points
play, obey, employ, say	plays, obeys, employs, says	played, obeyed, employed	y after vowel (a,e,i, o,u) just adds s, ed
cry, tidy, worry, fly	cries, tidies, worries, flies	cried, tidied, worried	drop y after consonant, add ies, ied

Arrange the following verbs into two groups according to the spelling of the 3rd person singular present simple tense (some have irregular past tenses).

(a) like *play: plays* (just add 's')
(b) like *cry: cries* (drop 'y', add 'ies')

stay	**copy**	**marry**	**display**	**buy**
carry	**destroy**	**occupy**	**multiply**	**dry**

Put the verbs in brackets into the 3rd person singular present simple.

(c) In the city everyone (hurry) everywhere and (try) to earn a lot of money. Someone in the country (enjoy) the peace and quiet of nature.
(d) A man who (spy) against his own country (betray) his own people and, if he is caught, (pay) with his life.

Put the verbs in brackets into the 'ed' form (past simple or past participle).

(e) The man said the train for Leeds was (delay) until they were (satisfy) that the track was safe.
(f) I (apply) for the job, and was (annoy) when they said that I was not (qualify) for it.

Spelling: 'ing' form and regular 'ed' past tense/past participle

One-syllable verbs			
Verbs	**'ing' form**	**Regular 'ed' form**	**Points**
wait, help, rain	waiting, helping, raining	waited, helped, rained	most verbs just add *ing, ed*
stop, stir, swim	stopping, stirring, swimming	stopped, stirred	final single consonant after one vowel doubles
write, care, hope, come	writing, caring, hoping, coming	cared, hoped	final single *e* after consonant is dropped
lie, die, tie	lying, dying, tying		final *ie* replaced with *y*
Note: *y, w, x* are never doubled, e.g. staying, stayed, blowing, boxing, boxed			

Arrange the following verbs into three groups according to the spelling of the 'ing' form.

(a) like *wait: waiting* (add '*ing*')
(b) like *stop: stopping* (double final consonant, add '*ing*')
(c) like *write: writing* (drop *e*, add '*ing*')

sleep	**get**	**give**	**close**	**hit**	**read**
put	**bore**	**dig**	**fail**	**cure**	**trim**
lose	**wear**	**clean**	**win**	**wipe**	**plug**
need	**shut**	**drop**	**start**	**score**	**lean**

In the first group of sentences below put the verbs in brackets into the 'ing' form. In the second group put the verbs into the regular 'ed' form.

(d) John's (sit) in the (live)-room, (watch) television and (eat) a sandwich. The dog is (lie) at his feet. I'm (cut) some more sandwiches.
(e) She (slow) down, (stop), (rub) her eyes and (stare) at the tall man who had (shout) and (step) out in front of her.

Instructions as above.

(f) We're (have) a party on Saturday. We're (look) forward to (see) you there. We've been (plan) it for weeks. We're (die) to see you again.
(g) That night she (phone) me. In a (tire) voice, she (beg) me not to leave her. 'I'm (scare). Don't go. I . . .' She (pause).

Two-syllable verbs ending in *one* consonant after *one* vowel			
Verbs	**'ing' form**	**Regular 'ed' form**	**Points**
listen, answer, visit	listening, answering, visiting	listened, answered, visited	stress on *first* syllable: just add *ing, ed*
	Main exception: final *l*, e.g. travelling, travelled		
begin, prefer, regret	beginning, preferring, regretting	preferred, regretted	stress on *second* syllable: double final consonant
	Note: *y,w,x* never doubled, e.g. obeying, allowed, relaxed		

Write the verbs in brackets in the correct 'ing' form'. The stress is given.

(a) Catherine's (begin) her new job tomorrow.
(b) Listen to that noise! What's (happen)?
(c) He spends a lot of time (travel) abroad.
(d) They're (open) a new shop in Oxford next month.
(e) I apologize for (forget) your birthday.
(f) Canada is now (permit) tourists to enter the country without visas.
(g) He's (sharpen) his pencils.
(h) I like to spend my holidays (relax) on the beach.

Write the verbs in brackets in the correct past tense. The stress is given.
(i) My grandfather (suffer) from very bad headaches.
(j) She said she (prefer) coffee to tea.
(k) The firm (allow) the workers to go home early during the very hot weather.
(l) When they heard I was ill, they (cancel) the meeting.
(m) He (admit) to the police that he had stolen the money.
(n) I (offer) him some money, but he wasn't interested.
(o) She (regret) that she couldn't come with us.
(p) Luckily no-one was in the house when the explosion (occur).

Spelling: miscellaneous points

1

Words	Points
also, almost, although, already, altogether, always etc.	only one *l*
careful, useful, awful, wonderful, helpful, successful etc.	only one *l*
taught (past of 'teach') caught (past of 'catch')	*au* not *ou*

Complete the correct spelling of the incomplete words.

(a) Al ____ gh it was raining, we decided to go for a walk.
(b) He has three sons and two daughters, that's five children al ____ er.
(c) I'm al ____ s tired, doctor. I never have any energy.
(d) She's al ____ y finished. Wasn't she quick?
(e) I've known him al ____ t all my life.
(f) What a won ____ l present! Thank you very much.
(g) The weather was aw ____ l. It was cold, wet and windy.
(h) Thank you for being so he ____ l when I was in trouble.
(i) I find a typewriter very us ____ l in my work.
(j) This work isn't very good. Please be more ca ____ l.
(k) This year our teacher is Miss Harley. Last year Mr Weeks t ____ t us.
(l) I missed the 10.15 train, but I c ____ t the 10.25.

2

Words	Points
whose, who's	*whose* = of whom (*Whose* pen is this?) *who's* = who is (*Who's* at the door?)
its, it's	*its* = of it (The dog ate *its* food) *it's* = it is (*It's* hot today.)
four, fourteen, forty	note *or* in *forty*

Choose the correct item in each pair.

(a) A woman (whose, who's) husband is dead is called a widow.
(b) (Whose, Who's) at the door? Can you go and see, please?
(c) I don't know (whose, who's) money this is.
(d) I don't know (whose, who's) coming to the party.
(e) Students (whose, who's) results are bad must take the exam again.
(f) She's very interested in Brazil and (its, it's) history.
(g) (Its, It's) very hot today, isn't it?
(h) I knew it was a giraffe because of (its, it's) long neck.
(i) The firm has decided to change (its, it's) name.
(j) I think (its, it's) going to rain.

Spell these numbers: (k) 4 (l) 14 (m) 40 (n) 44

3

Words	Points
necessary, accommodation, address, success, possible, different, etc.	note double consonants
copier, dirtiest, laziness, happily, beautiful etc.	final *y* after consonant changes to *i* before *er, est, ness, ly, ful*
system, mystery, pyramid, etc.	note: *y* not *i*

Put in the missing double letters in the incomplete words.

(a) Is it po __ ible to take a di __ erent train?
(b) Can you give me any a __ re __ es of student a __ o __ odation?
(c) Hard work, not luck, is nece __ ary for examination su __ e __ .

Make a suitable word from each word in brackets.

(d) He's very lazy. He's the (lazy) person I know.
(e) It's a very (beauty) part of the country.
(f) We have a very good photo-(copy) in our office.
(g) The birth of their daughter brought them a lot of (happy).
(h) I think the streets are (dirty) now than they were ten years ago.

Put the missing letter in each word in brackets.

(i) The police don't know what happened. It's a complete (m__stery).
(j) Tokyo has a very good public transport (s__stem).
(k) Have you seen the (p__ramids) of Egypt?

4

Words (silent letter in brackets)	Words (silent letter in brackets)
guard, guess etc. (u)	school, character etc. (h)
climb, comb etc. (b)	knee, knife etc. (k)
doubt, debt etc. (b)	autumn, column etc. (n)
exhibition, exhausted etc. (h)	receipt, psychological etc. (p)
hour, honest etc. (h)	write, wrong etc. (w)

Put in the missing silent letters in each incomplete word.

(a) Did you com__ your hair before you went to sc__ool this morning?
(b) Of course we were ex__austed after clim__ing the mountain.
(c) That's our first g__est __nocking at the door.
(d) I think autum__ is the __rong time to go there. Summer is better.
(e) We need an __onest man with a good c__aracter.
(f) The assistant forgot to give me a recei__t when I bought the g__itar.
(g) There is no dou__t that it is the best ex__ibition for years.
(h) She cut her __nee with a __nife.
(i) It took me an __our to __rite the letter.

Key

Topics

The Weather (p.5) 1 (a) forecast (b) fog (c) mist
(d) rain (e) snow (f) wind (g) cloud (h) sun
2 (a) changeable (b) wet (c) dry (d) clear (e) cloudy
(f) hot (g) warm (h) mild (i) cold (j) freezing **3** (a) 2 (b) 4
(c) 6 (d) 3 (e) 1 (f) 5
Going Shopping (p.6) 1 (a) manager (b) cashier
(c) till (d) customers (e) check-out (f) queue (g) trolley
(h) basket (i) shelves (j) assistant **2** (a) spend (b) need
(c) buy (d) sell (e) push (f) look for (g) find (h) take
(i) pay (j) complain **3** (a) round (b) for (c) at (d) in front of
(e) on (f) for (g) from (h) in (i) in (j) to **4** (a) packet
(b) bottle (c) tube (d) box (e) carton (f) jar (g) tin
(h) bottle (i) box (j) bottle, tube (k) carton, tin, bottle
(l) jar, tube (m) jar (n) tin (o) jar (p) packet (q) packet
(r) tin, tube (s) packet **5** (a) 3 (b) 7 (c) 4 (d) 1 (e) 6 (f) 5
(g) 2
Work (p.8) 1 (a) 7 (b) 5 (c) 6 (d) 1 (e) 2 (f) 3 (g) 4
2 (a) interview (b) experience (c) qualifications (d) skills
(e) personal qualities (f) wages (g) hours **3** (a) 3 (b) 5
(c) 6 (d) 2 (e) 7 (f) 1 (g) 4 **4** (a) footballer (b) farmer
(c) actress (d) librarian (e) labourer (f) secretary
(g) lawyer (h) porter (i) journalist (j) mechanic
(k) businessman (l) priest (m) waiter (n) carpenter
(o) scientist
Education (p.10) 1 (a) play-school (b) learn (c) start
(d) compulsory (e) primary school (f) terms (g) pupils
(h) mixed (i) staff **2** (a) secondary school (b) state school
(c) private school (d) subjects (e) specialize (f) take
(g) pass (h) marks (i) fail **3** (a) student (b) grant (c) fees
(d) keen (e) studies (f) courses (g) last (h) graduate
(i) degree **4** (a) graduate (b) teacher training college
(c) classes (d) lessons (e) homework (f) mark (g) prepare
(h) behave (i) strict **5** (a) at (b) at (c) in (d) on (e) to
(f) with (g) at (h) from (i) to, in (j) of (k) of (l) in
(m) between (n) with
Money (p.12) 1 (a) earn (b) spend (c) borrow (d) lend
(e) open (f) save (g) pay (h) afford (i) pay back (j) owe
2 (a) well-off (b) hard-up (c) make ends meet (d) broke
(e) in debt **3** (a) from (b) on (c) on (d) in **4** (a) 3 (b) 4
(c) 7 (d) 1 (e) 10 (f) 8 (g) 5 (h) 9 (i) 2 (j) 6. *Income*: b, c,
f, g, h; *Expenditure*: a, d, e, i, j.
A Life (p.14) 1 (a) was born (b) come from (c) grow
up (d) bring up (e) educate (f) move (g) join (h) leave
(i) become (j) settle down **2** (a) in (b) in (c) from (d) in
(e) in (f) at (g) in (h) as **3** (a) 4 (b) 5 (c) 1 (d) 6 (e) 2 (f) 3
Sport (p.16) 1 (a) 3 (b) 1 (c) 7 (d) 5 (e) 9 (f) 8 (g) 4
(h) 6 (i) 2 **2** (a) play (b) train (c) win (d) lose (e) draw
(f) beat (g) score **3** (a) two nil (b) four all (c) nil all
(d) thirty love (e) fifteen all (f) love fifteen **4** (a) shooting
(b) table-tennis (c) basketball (d) skating (e) football
(f) motor-racing (g) running (h) baseball (i) cricket
(j) rugby (k) boxing (l) volley-ball (m) cycling (n) golf
(o) fishing (p) tennis (q) horse-riding (r) badminton
(s) skiing (t) swimming (u) hockey **5** (1) k (2) g (3) f (4) a
(5) s (6) r (7) (c) (8) g (9) q (10) t (11) i (12) f (13) h
(14) h (15) d (16) a (17) e (18) u (19) o (20) p (21) e
(22) h (23) c/e/l/p (24) t (25) r (26) n (27) j (28) c (29) k
(30) m
Free Time and Holidays (p.18) 1 (a) parties
(b) sociable (c) dancing (d) meeting people (e) clubs
(f) discos (g) go by plane (h) hotel (i) have a good time

(j) sunbathe **2** (a) cultural things (b) serious (c) classical
music (d) reading (e) concerts (f) libraries (g) hitch-hike
(h) youth hostels (i) learn about other countries (j) visit
historical places **3** (a) the open air (b) active (c) sport
(d) nature (e) sporting events (f) the countryside (g) take
a train (h) camp sites (i) be close to nature (j) go for
walks **4** (a) to (b) at (c) on (d) on (e) at (f) to (g) at
(h) about (i) of (j) at (k) to (l) by
Illness and the Doctor (p.20) 1 (a) chemist
(b) doctor (c) patient (d) nurse (e) receptionist (f) brain
(g) lungs (h) heart (i) stomach **2** (a) examine (b) treat
(c) suffer (d) cure (e) operate (f) look after (g) keep
(h) ache **3** (a) in (b) to (c) for (d) to (e) to (f) with (g) on
4 (a) 4 (b) 3 (c) 6 (d) 1 (e) 7 (f) 2 (g) 8 (h) 5
In the Morning (p.22) 1 (a) shower (b) comb
(c) briefcase (d) soap (e) hairbrush (f) newspaper
(g) shaver (h) alarm clock (i) toothbrush (j) teeth
(k) clothes (l) pyjamas **2** d,f,h,b,j,c,a,r,k,e,q,g,n,i,o,p,l,m
3 (a) wear (b) put on (c) dress (d) put on (e) wear
(f) dress
The Telephone (p.24) 1 (a) 2 (b) 3 (c) 5 (d) 1 (e) 4
2 (a) 4 (b) 6 (c) 5 (d) 8 (e) 9 (f) 1 (g) 7 (h) 2 (i) 3 (j) 11
(k) 10 **3** (a) wrong number (b) engaged (c) long-distance
(d) rates (e) operator (f) off-peak (g) interference
(h) directory (i) directory enquiries (j) call-box (k) receiver
Watching Television (p.25) 1(a) 5 (b) 3 (c) 6 (d) 9
(e) 4 (f) 2 (g) 7 (h) 1 (i) 8 **3** (a) turn off (b) record (c) turn
on (d) switch (e) plan (f) look up

How to Do Things

How to Do the Washing Up (p.26) 1(a) tap (b) sink
(c) cloth (d) draining-board (e) drawer (f) brush
(g) sponge (h) dishes (i) cupboard (j) washing-up liquid
2 (2) turn on, fill, turn off (3) add (5) rinse (6) drain
(7) dry (8) put away
How to Make an English Breakfast (p.27)
1 (a) toaster (b) napkin (c) frying-pan (d) teapot (e) bowl
(f) salt (g) jug (h) tea-bag (i) glass (j) table-cloth
(k) pepper (l) kettle **2** (1) lay (2) boil (3) pour (4) add, stir
(5) spread (6) fry (8) clear away
How to Do Keep-Fit Exercises (p.28) 1 (1) stand,
hang (2) raise (3) turn, move (3) lower **2** (2) hold (3) lean
(4) bend, bring, touch (5) straighten
How to Use a Cassette Player (p.29) 1 (a) switch
(b) batteries (c) lead (d) point (e) knob (f) plug (g) button
(h) controls **2** (1) plug in (2) switch on (3) press (4) turn
down, turn (5) turn up (8) switch off (9) unplug

Related Word Groups

Basic Adjectives (p.30) 1(a) 5 (b) 3 (c) 2 (d) 4 (e) 1
2 (a) 3 (b) 1 (c) 4 (d) 5 (e) 2 **3** (a) 4 (b) 5 (c) 2 (d) 1 (e) 3
4 (a) 5 (b) 4 (c) 2 (d) 3 (e) 1 **5** (a) 3 (b) 5 (c) 1 (d) 2 (e) 4
6 (a) 2 (b) 1 (c) 4 (d) 5 (e) 3
Basic Adjectives: opposites (p.31) 1(a) good
(b) fat (c) thick (d) late (e) deep (f) hot **2** (a) heavy
(b) dark (c) young (d) casual (e) major (f) new **3** (a) small
(b) wide (c) busy (d) wealthy (e) smooth (f) calm
4 (a) blunt (b) safe (c) public (d) wonderful (e) clean

(f) short **5** (a) empty (b) guilty (c) easy (d) huge (e) tight
(f) low **6** (a) slow (b) nice (c) cheap (d) wrong (e) weak
(f) dry **7** (a) stupid (b) sad (c) rude (d) soft (e) ugly (f) quiet
Verbs (p.32) **1**(a) 4 (b) 1 (c) 5 (d) 3 (e) 2 **2** (a) 4 (b) 3
(c) 5 (d) 1 (e) 2 **3** (a) 3 (b) 5 (c) 2 (d) 1 (e) 4 **4** (a) 2 (b) 1
(c) 4 (d) 5 (e) 3 **5** (a) 3 (b) 5 (c) 4 (d) 1 (e) 2
Action Verbs (p.33) **1**(a) driver (b) cleaner (c) artist
(d) athlete (e) hairdresser (f) dressmaker (g) hairdresser
(h) cleaner (i) athlete (j) dressmaker (k) artist (l) driver
2 (a) dentist (b) soldier (c) pilot (d) gardener (e) postman
(f) teacher (g) teacher (h) postman (i) soldier (j) gardener
(k) pilot (l) dentist
Adjectives Describing Character (p.34)
1 (a) sociable (b) adventurous (c) impatient **2** (a) easy-
going (b) talkative (c) ambitious **3** (a) naughty (b) lazy
(c) cheerful **4** (a) selfish (b) sensible (c) optimistic
5 (a) tidy (b) polite (c) imaginative **6** (a) polite (b) lazy
(c) sensible (d) optimistic (e) sociable (f) cheerful
(g) naughty (h) impatient (i) talkative (j) tidy (k) easy-
going (l) ambitious (m) adventurous (n) selfish
(o) imaginative
People's Appearance (p.35) **1** (a) short (b) elderly
(c) bald (d) glasses (e) his arms folded (f) well-dressed
(g) striped (h) well-pressed (i) well-polished shoes
(a) strongly-built (b) in his thirties (c) straight (d) bracelet
(e) his hands on his hips (f) casually-dressed
(g) checked (h) patched (i) trainers **2** (a) slim (b) middle-
aged (c) wavy (d) necklace (e) her hands clasped
(f) neatly-dressed (g) spotted (h) smart (i) high-heeled
shoes (a) average height (b) teenage (c) curly (d) bow
(e) her hands by her sides (f) untidily-dressed (g) plain
(h) baggy (i) sandals
Materials (p.37) (a) wool (b) glass (c) paper
(d) cotton (e) denim (f) stone (g) leather (h) metal
(i) brick (j) plastic (k) wood (l) iron (m) steel (n) china
(o) rubber
Geographical Words (p.37) (a) 4 (b) 8 (c) 1 (d) 5
(e) 9 (f) 2 (g) 3 (h) 11 (i) 7 (j) 12 (k) 6 (l) 10

Word Building

'ful' and 'less' (p.38) (a) useful (b) useless (c) painless
(d) painful (e) homeless (f) helpful (g) sleepless
(h) hopeful (i) tasteless
'Interesting' and 'Interested' etc. (p.38)
(a) exciting (b) excited (c) relaxed (d) relaxing
(e) satisfied (f) satisfying (g) boring (h) bored
(i) frightened (j) frightening (k) annoying (l) annoyed
'er' and 'or' (p.39) (a) worker (b) visitor (c) cleaner
(d) actor (e) driver (f) employer (g) manager (h) director
(i) operator (j) maker (k) painter (l) builder (m) collector
(n) sailor (o) speaker
'ist' and 'an' (p.39) (a) Christian (b) typist (c) politician
(d) American (e) pianist (f) scientist (g) electrician
(h) cyclist (i) artist (j) guitarist (k) Roman (l) novelist
'Hourly', 'Daily' etc. (p.39) (a) daily (b) weekly
(c) yearly (d) hourly (e) fortnightly (f) monthly
'en' (p.40) (a) tighten (b) loosen (c) brighten
(d) sharpen (e) deafen (f) widen (g) lengthen
(h) strengthen
Number+Noun (p.40) (a) five-mile (b) ten-minute
(c) 200-page (d) 20-storey (e) two-week (f) ten-metre
(g) six-month (h) five-country (i) two-ton
'un', 'dis', 'in', 'im', 'il', 'ir' (p.41) **1** (a) unwell
(b) unnecessary (c) unhealthy (d) unpleasant
(e) unemployed (f) unpunctual (g) unfair **2** (a) untidy
(b) unfriendly (c) unsatisfactory (d) unusual

(e) unconscious (f) unsuccessful (g) unhurt **3** (a) unlock
(b) unpack (c) untie (d) unwrap (e) undo (f) undress
4 (a) irregular (b) incorrect (c) illegal (d) inconvenient
(e) impolite (f) informal (g) dishonest
Adverbs of Manner (p.42) (a) stupidly
(b) continuously (c) heroically (d) noisily (e) truthfully
(f) dramatically (g) hard (h) angrily (i) publicly
(j) strangely (k) tidily (l) completely, absolutely
Compound Nouns (p.43) **1** (a) a birthday-party (b) a
question-mark (c) a college library (d) a university
student (e) office furniture (f) work clothes (g) a lorry-
driver (h) a television programme (i) a government
building (j) an evening class (k) a shop-window (l) a
bread-knife (m) exercise-book (n) ticket inspector
(o) toothbrush (p) stamp-album (q) road-map (r) shoe-
lace (s) orange-juice (t) book-list (u) film magazine
(v) camera shop (w) tourist bus **2** (a) stamp collections
(b) city-centres (c) teacups (d) concert-halls (e) family
doctors (f) picture-frames (g) dog owners (h) car-wheels
(i) airline pilots (j) matchboxes
Word Forms (p.44) (1) decision, decide
(2) congratulate, congratulations (3) permit, permission
(4) invitation, invite (5) arrival, arrive (6) depart,
departure (7) complain, complaint (8) argue, argument
(9) importance, important (10) difficult, difficulty
(11) height, high (12) arrangement, arrange (13) bleed,
blood (14) practice, practise (15) description, describe
(16) explanation, explain (17) enjoy, enjoyable (18) fly,
flight (19) signature, sign (20) meet, meeting (21) hot,
heat (22) suit, suitable (23) relaxation, relax (24) choose,
choice (25) legal, legalize (26) modernize, modern
(27) industry, industrial (28) agricultural, agriculture
(29) simple, simplify (30) admit, admission (31) freedom,
free (32) weigh, weight (33) noisy, noise (34) safety, safe
(35) dangerous, danger (36) peace, peaceful (37) lose,
loss (38) mix, mixture (39) dirty, dirt (40) violent, violence
(41) measurement, measure (42) kind, kindness
(43a) happily (b) happy (c) happiness (44a) success
(b) succeed (c) successful (45a) die (b) dead (c) death

Idioms

Verb Phrases (p.47) **1** (a) make your bed (b) make a
list (c) make an appointment (d) make your breakfast
(e) make sure (f) make a noise **2** (a) make a decision
(b) make enquiries (c) make plans (d) make some
money (e) make friends (f) make an effort **3** (a) take
care (b) take a photo (c) take an exam (d) take a seat
(e) take any notice (f) take place **4** (a) have a bath
(b) have breakfast (c) have a game of tennis (d) have
fun (e) have a party (f) have a rest **5** (a) keep fit (b) keep
still (c) keep calm (d) keep a record (e) keep awake
(f) keep quiet **6** (a) do my shopping (b) do the
housework (c) do some work (d) do exercises (e) do me
good (f) do a lot of harm **7** (a) get married (b) get a lot of
money (c) get flu (d) get a train (e) get ready
'Touch' (p.49) (a) keep in touch (b) get out of touch
(c) get in touch
Prepositional Phrases (p.49) **1** (a) at home (b) at
work (c) at the sea side (d) at school (e) at first (f) at
least (g) at once (h) at last **2** (a) on time (b) on fire (c) on
foot (d) on holiday (e) on business (f) on the one hand
(g) on the other hand (h) on second thoughts **3** (a) in
person (b) in time (c) in prison (d) in a mess (e) in
trouble (f) in love (g) in tears (h) in a hurry **4** (a) by
mistake (b) by post (c) by phone (d) by chance (e) by
car (f) by bus (g) by all means (h) by the way **5** (a) out of

date (b) out of doors (c) out of order (d) out of control
(e) out of breath (f) out of work

Pairs (p.51) **1** (a) more or less (b) so and so (c) on
and off (d) yes and no **2** (a) likes and dislikes (b) little by
little (c) do's and don'ts (d) peace and quiet

Time (p.51) (a) ages (b) the other day (c) so far
(d) from now on (e) one day (f) for good

'Mind' (p.52) (a) in two minds (b) change your mind
(c) make up your mind (d) mind your head (e) I don't
mind

Things We Say (p.52) **1** (a) 4 (b) 3 (c) 2 (d) 1 **2** (a) 4
(b) 1 (c) 2 (d) 3 **3** (a) 4 (b) 3 (c) 2 (d) 1 **4** (a) 2 (b) 3 (c) 1
(d) 4

Miscellaneous

Abbreviations (p.53) **1** (a) a.m. (b) p.m. (c) etc.
(d) e.g. (e) NB (f) PS (g) US (h) c/o (i) Rd (j) PTO **2** (a) ft
(b) ins (c) lbs (d) BC (e) AD (f) i.e. (g) EEC (h) UK
(i) USSR

Reading Dates and Numbers (p.55) **1** (a) . . . 6th
April (*or*: April 6) 1743 (b) . . . £2.35 (c) . . . 370 4492
(d) . . . 1276 (e) 1cm=0.3937 ins **2** (a) . . . the fourth of
May nineteen thirty-seven (b) . . . four pounds fifty each
(c) four oh eight nine double-one seven (d) . . . twelve
thousand seven hundred and fifty pounds (e) one pound
is (*or*: equals) nought point four five four kilograms

Punctuation Marks (p.55) (a) inverted commas
(b) exclamation mark (c) full stop (d) question mark
(e) capital letter (f) small letter (g) apostrophe (h) hyphen
(i) comma (j) brackets

Spelling: noun plurals (p.56) **1** (a) wishes, kisses
(b) boxes, matches (c) watches, dresses (d) boys,
studies (e) toys, countries (f) libraries, Sundays
(g) families, monkeys, ways, babies (h) sheep (i) fish
2 (a) yourselves, knives (b) wives, handkerchiefs
(c) lives, roofs (d) kilos, tomatoes (e) photos, heroes
(f) women, feet (g) children, teeth

Spelling: verbs ending in 'y' (p.57) (a) stay,
destroy, display, buy (b) carry, copy, marry, occupy,
multiply, dry (c) hurries, tries, enjoys (d) spies, betrays,
pays (e) delayed, satisfied (f) applied, annoyed, qualified

**Spelling: 'ing' form and regular 'ed' past tense/
past participle (p.58)** **1** (a) sleep, need, wear, clean,
fall, start, read, lean (b) put, get, shut, dig, drop, win, hit,
trim, plug (c) lose, bore, give, close, cure, wipe, score
(d) sitting, living, watching, eating, lying, cutting
(e) slowed, stopped, rubbed, stared, shouted, stepped
(f) having, looking, seeing, planning, dying (g) phoned,
tired, begged, scared, paused **2** (a) beginning
(b) happening (c) travelling (d) opening (e) forgetting
(f) permitting (g) sharpening (h) relaxing (i) suffered
(j) preferred (k) allowed (l) cancelled (m) admitted
(n) offered (o) regretted (p) occurred

Spelling: miscellaneous points (p.60)
1 (a) although (b) altogether (c) always (d) already
(e) almost (f) wonderful (g) awful (h) helpful (i) useful
(j) careful (k) taught (l) caught **2** (a) whose (b) who's
(c) whose (d) who's (e) whose (f) its (g) it's (h) its (i) its
(j) it's (k) four (l) fourteen (m) forty (n) forty-four
3 (a) possible, different (b) addresses, accommodation
(c) necessary, success (d) laziest (e) beautiful (f) copier
(g) happiness (h) dirtier (i) mystery (j) system
(k) pyramids **4** (a) comb, school (b) exhausted, climbing
(c) guest, knocking (d) autumn, wrong (e) honest,
character (f) receipt, guitar (g) doubt, exhibition (h) knee,
knife (i) hour, write